THE FIRST DAY
OF ETERNITY

George A. Maloney, S.J.

THE FIRST DAY OF ETERNITY

Resurrection Now

CROSSROAD · NEW YORK

1982
The Crossroad Publishing Company
575 Lexington Avenue, New York, NY 10022

Library of Congress Cataloging in Publication Data

Maloney, George A., 1924–
The first day of eternity.

1. Jesus Christ—Resurrection. 2. Resurrection.
I. Title.
BT481.M34   232'.5   82–17250
ISBN 0–8245–0445–3   AACR2

To Hallie and Delene Brown

CONTENTS

THE FIRST DAY
OF ETERNITY

PREFACE

A Chinese proverb expresses what this book is about:

> There's the man who
> doesn't know that
> he doesn't know—
> He's a fool, avoid him.
>
> There's the man who
> knows that he doesn't know.
> He's ignorant, teach him.
>
> There's the man who
> doesn't know that he knows.
> He's asleep, awake him.
>
> There's the man who
> knows that he knows.
> He is wise, listen to him.

There are various degrees of "knowing" about resurrection. But the highest level of knowing the resurrection is to be led into the mystery that is at the heart of all reality—love. Whether it be your love for God or for another human person, you know in that awesome experience that you have attained a knowledge beyond your own rational knowledge. You have been ushered into a deep cavern of darkness. But as you learn to let go of your control over the reality around you, the darkness begins to be illumined with soft lights. You "see" now what always had been there in that dark cavern but somehow was hidden.

The experience of resurrection is at the source of all reality. It is love moving out of self-controlled reason to trustful abandonment as you take the risk to "believe" that in losing your life you find it in greater abundance in loving union with another through a dying process.

Meaning of Resurrection

The essential doctrine that makes Christianity the most unique religion in man's history is that of the resurrection.

> But Christ has in fact been raised from the dead, the first-fruits of all who have fallen asleep. Death came through one man and in the same way the resurrection of the dead has come through one man. Just as all men die in Adam, so all men will be brought to life in Christ. (1 Cor 15:20–22)

Yet what does resurrection mean for us today? Because it is an experience of mystery, it admits of many meanings and interpretations.

If we consult any dictionary for the meaning of the resurrection, we shall usually find first that it refers to the rising again of Christ after His death and burial. It will also refer to the rising again of all of us at the Last Day. We have an habitual picture in our imagination when we hear the word *resurrection*. We imagine that the dead body of Jesus was taken down from the cross on Good Friday and laid in the tomb, that it lay there for three days and that the resurrection took place the moment His soul returned to that tomb and entered again into that cold cadaver. Jesus became the same, conscious living person who had died on the cross. He disentangled Himself from the linen cloths and walked out of the tomb. During the following forty days He appeared to His disciples, ate meals with them and even invited them to touch Him to reassure themselves that He was really risen. Then He finally met with them and blessed them as he ascended into the heavens to sit at the right hand of the Father.

Our true understanding of Christ's resurrection and its meaning for us must be rooted in the historicity of the first community of believers. How did they understand Christ's resurrection with its repercussions on their lives? The faith experience of the resurrection in the early Christian community as recorded in the Gospels and the other New Testament writings must be the ground for our faith in the full meaning of the resurrection. Yet faith goes beyond historical criticism. The latter can unfold to us how Jesus' disciples came to believe.

But resurrection as an event that happened to the historical Jesus of Nazareth cannot be verified by historical methods. Historical criticism can establish only that Jesus died and that the early disciples witnessed to His appearances and came to believe in Him as risen. Faith, a gift from the Spirit of the risen Jesus, allows us in mystery to approach the resurrection as a statement about the death of Jesus whom the Heavenly Father raised up to glory and gave the power to bring new life and hope to all human beings. The New Testament does not explain to our reasoning powers why the death of Jesus should have been necessary to new life. It merely states the necessity which is to be accepted and lived on faith. "Was it not ordained that the Christ should suffer and so enter into his glory?" (Lk 24:26)

Faith invites us to enter into that faith-community and, united with those early believers in the breaking of the bread, to experience the death-resurrection of Christ in a community of dying and rising people.

Meaningfulness before Death

Today we are plagued with the problem of the meaning of our human existence before mounting invisible powers of evil in our society along with our burden of guilt for the disharmony within ourselves and around us in the world. Death threatens any meaningful existence. With so much to live for, we want to live longer than previous human beings did. But through technology we see more of death all about us. Hence our preoccupation with the problem of death and dying as we search for higher levels of consciousness contributing greater ultimate meaningfulness to life.

Jesus lived and taught that in order to attain the full, true human life and to share in God's eternal life, self-centeredness had to be abandoned. He lived for others and freely died for all of us. He shows us an image of God emptying Himself out in the nature of a servant. Saint Paul shows us the reason for Christ's death: ". . . and the reason he died for all was so that living men should live no longer for themselves, but for him who died and was raised to life for them" (2 Cor 5:15). As death out of love for us brought Jesus' resurrection, so the pattern for the Christian life is the same: we must die to sin in order to live in a newness of life. "If in union with Christ we have imitated his death, we shall also imitate him in his resurrection. We must realize that our former selves have been crucified with him to destroy this sinful body and to free us from the slavery of sin" (Rom 6:5–6).

Jesus has taken the sting out of death and given us meaningfulness beyond this life that stretches into eternal life. He has "broken the power of death" (2 Tm 1:10). The Good News is that God so loved this world as to give us His only Son that we might believe in Him as the saving Lord and thus share in God's eternal life (Jn 3:16). God's love is the ultimate meaningfulness beyond all man-made, rational explanations of what is really real. But this is a love that is self-emptying, *kenotic* in its outpouring of oneself in self-sacrifice for the other. No rational assault upon life's ultimate meaning can ever effect a surrender of the mystery of love that covers itself only with darkness when man's mere probing intellect attacks.

And yet to the broken ones of this world who humbly cry out to God for the coming of His Love incarnated, Jesus Christ, into their lives, this mystery of love that *death is resurrection*, is revealed. It becomes a living experience that cannot be taught and yet that grows into the fullness of reality as one enters into the *exodus-passover* experience of moving away from self-centeredness to God-centeredness.

Entering into Mystery

This is a book in which I humbly seek to present the message of the resurrection of Jesus and our own participation as a mystery. Let us struggle prayerfully together to de-objectivize our habitual understanding of the resurrection of Jesus and our own personal resurrection. It takes great courage and faith to give up our own view of a personal, bodily resurrection that can be so often loaded with selfishness and gross concession to self-glorification and can distort the true message of Jesus and His early disciples concerning resurrection.

Let us seriously ask how we can *now*, in the present moment in our broken history in time and space, experience it as a part of the whole that began on the "third day" of Easter and will reach its full fruition on the "Last Day." Past speculation about what happened historically to Jesus has little power to convert us today to live in the paschal victory of Jesus Christ. Future speculation about what we shall be like when we rise from our graves and details of how Christ will appear in the glory of His second coming can all too often take us away from the present urgency to commit ourselves *now* to the risen Lord, present in our broken world, as He seeks to invite us to a reconciliation of this world to His Father.

Is Christ Really Risen?

Christians too long have conceived the resurrection of Jesus in the past and our own resurrection as an event in the future. By such objectivizing, we strip the resurrection of its mystery and hence its power to be a living issue and a fundamental choice that we are called to make *now* in the context of our daily lives.

Intellectually we give an assent that we call faith to the abstract truth that Jesus Christ has risen from the dead. But does such faith become a burning, grappling decision to discover Him at each moment of our lives being risen from the dead in the context of our present, broken world, suffocating from its bondage to "sin and death"? Are we as Christians living lives in our contemporary society that are any different from those lived by humanists, atheists, Muslims, Hindus or Buddhists? Does the reality of the historical Jesus who died and was raised by God unto glory give us a different Christ-consciousness from that induced by the latest techniques on mind-expansion and marketed so promisingly by innumerable seminars and workshops throughout our gullible land?

If Christ *is* the resurrection, should this reality not be a daily experience for us Christians? Should this reality not make us completely different from non-Christians?

One of my favorite scenes in the Gospels is that of Jesus speaking to Martha before the tomb of His friend, Lazarus. It best expresses why I wrote this book. Martha, the busy doer in the kitchen, worrying about many things (Lk 10:41), typifies in a way our Western mentality. She believed her brother would rise again at the resurrection on the last day (Jn 11:25). She failed to see that before her stood He who *is* the resurrection. He is "the Way, the Truth and the Life" (Jn 14:6). He has come into our world to bring us life, that we might always have it more abundantly (Jn10:10). He is the Bread of life (Jn 6:35). Whoever believes in Him shall enjoy eternal life (Jn 6:40) right now, even though he will face a physical death later on.

And so the risen Jesus is facing all of us as He tells Martha:

I am the resurrection.
If anyone believes in me,
even though he dies he will live,
and whoever lives and believes in me
will never die.
Do you believe this?

Jn 11:15–26

Martha gives what should be our answer and our experience in the context of daily living: "Yes, Lord, I believe that you are the Christ, the Son of God, the one who was to come into this world" (Jn 11:27).

God's Miracle

The resurrection is God's constant miracle meeting us in the sordid brokenness, but also in the limited joys and moments of self-fullfillment, in the many deaths and risings from the dead that make up the story of this day and of tomorrow and of every day of our earthly existence. Jesus in His Body of which we are His members can be raised in this moment to newness of life. The resurrection of Jesus, the Head, of His Church, of the members, you and me as individuals, finding our uniqueness precisely by discovering ourselves in the corporateness of that Body, is *now* taking place as we unveil and yield to the power of the risen Lord in the context of our place and time in history.

The touch of the risen Lord can change the sufferings of body or mind or spirit that you are undergoing into a new sharing of His eternal life. The recent loss of your loved one can be a new release from selfish possession to loving and prayerful presence to him or her in a new union that passes from death to resurrection. Your financial worries and anxieties can be a death-to-new-life as you seek the Kingdom of God before all else and experience Christ's new resurrectional life.

Laughter and joy amidst apparent absurdity can be signs of not taking ourselves too seriously as candidates for the Godhead, but of experiencing God's raising power in our weakness.

Content of the Book

Our approach is to present the mystery of the resurrection of Jesus and our own sharing in it with a beginning prayerful consideration of God's call in history to His people. God's invitation to share His life with us reaches its climax in the New Testament when God's Word is enfleshed in the person of Jesus of Nazareth. He speaks of death-resurrection and lives it out, especially on the cross.

In the power of Jesus' *passover* from death to new life, we can now receive the Spirit of His love and enter into a new existence that destroys the limitations imposed upon our historical time and space by sin, death and the "elements of the world." We belong to Christ, the Victor, who has conquered sin and death.

In the experience of sharing, even *now*, in Christ's victory as we die to our selfishness and rise by the Spirit of love to live by loving service to others, we can examine both the meaning of suffering and our final physical death in the light of Christ's resurrection.

The Eucharist is contemplated as the fullness of redeemed time and space where we meet the full concentration of Christ, dying and rising for love of us as Victim-Gift and victorious Giver of eternal life. Such a sacramental symbol unleashes the power and glory of Jesus risen to allow us to be Eucharist and co-creators of the cosmos.

To experience the new life in Christ and to be able to bring that new creation to others, we need the Spirit of the risen Jesus. Guided by the interior presence of the Spirit, we can know how to do all actions to please God. We can take our place in the Body of Christ and build up the community of Jesus-people by developing in loving service the charisms the Spirit gives us.

The mystery of the Ascension highlights, not an objectivized "departure" of Christ from this world, but rather the ever, immanent presence of the risen Lord in our material world. He is *exalted* in glory means He is always among us sharing with us all power and glory to live in His Lordship.

Finally, we seek in the last chapter to bring together the mysterious and paradoxical realities of the *already* of Jesus, risen and effecting *now* our share in His resurrection, and the *not-yet* that awaits us on the Last Day. The hope in the full manifestation of Christ risen in glory, the Parousia, is a goal that we eagerly stretch out to possess in joy as we peacefully and lovingly work with Christ's Spirit to bring about the second coming of Christ in His glorified Body, His Church, at the end of time.

Other books can be consulted for a more scholarly treatment of what Scripture tells us of the resurrection of Christ and our own share in that resurrection. This work is not in competition with them. I offer it to you, reader, as a gathering together of "insights" about the mystery of the central reality of our Christian faith, the resurrection of Jesus and our own resurrection. May the Spirit of the risen Jesus Lord take these simple sparks and inflame in your heart a new exciting experience of what today could mean for you: the first day of eternity!

Chapter One

GOD CALLS HIS PEOPLE

At no other time in history has the human person lived in an environment of such mobility and fluidity as in our present epoch. Outer space has exploded our static concepts of our human potential and impells us to stretch out and never stop exploring the unknown beyond. What once took us five days of travel now can be telescoped by jet airliners into a few hours. At this moment we can be simultaneously present by satellite television to persons thousands of miles away and events that are happening tomorrow.

Yet are space and time only measurements of accomplishments done, or are they the backdrop against which we grow into our identity? The poet, W.H. Auden, well describes space and time in terms of meaningful, loving relationships:

> Space is the Whom our loves are needed by
> Time is our choice of How to love and Why.[1]

One of the great, modern prophets, who with blazing eyes pierces through the darkness and illusory values of this world and with rapier-pen calls us back to the inner, real world, is Alexander Solzhenitsyn. In his second volume of *The Gulag Archipelago*, he describes how he found the path to true inner freedom and enlightenment in a prison camp. Space and time at last became for him the persons for whom he lived to love and the choices he made as to how and why he loved.

> It was in my prison camp that for the first time I understood reality.
> It was there that I realized that the line between good and evil passes

9

not between countries, not between political parties, not between classes, but down, straight down each separate individual human heart. . . . It was on rotting straw in my labour camp that I learned this and I thank you, prison, for teaching me this truth.[2]

Placed in Time and Space

Our Christian teaching assures us in a faith-vision that our God is a loving, concerned God. We are not tossed into a time of history and a geographical place like flotsam on the ocean. God has called us into being in a historical time and place. There He promises to meet us and invite us to enter into a covenant friendship in order to share with us His very own life and being.

To be human is to hear God's continued call in the depths of our being, in what Scripture calls our heart. He calls us in a *vocation* to become more progressively, by the power of His Son and Holy Spirit, what we now are not. We are nomadic people stretching toward our true homeland, "living among foreigners in the Dispersion" (1 Pet 1:1) Yet we are called "by the provident purpose of God the Father to be made holy by the Spirit, obedient to Jesus Christ and sprinkled with his blood" (1 Pet 1:2).

Not only does He call us in every moment of each event "to share the divine nature" but He gives us the possibility of actualizing our divinization and thus "to escape corruption in a world that is sunk in vice" (2 Pet 1:4) He calls us to an ever ongoing conversion to give up our limited vision of Him in His loving activities of uncreated energies of love in order to enter deeply into the inner vision of reality to find Him at the heart of His material world.

God's Call

He calls us as He called Adam and Eve in the Garden of Eden to communicate with His Word in the Spirit of love. He allows us to share in the covenant He extended to Abraham at Haran (Gen 12:1–4; 15:1–21; 18:19) if we too are ready to give up all earthly possessions in order to obey God's will. God calls us as He called Moses (Ex 3:1–6), Isaiah (Is 6:5–7) and Jeremiah (Jer 1:4–8).

God's calling of individuals is His calling them to perform a work of cooperation to extend His eternal love to His collective people "of all nations." Thus God never calls an individual to share God's life alone but

He calls a people, the "called-out" assembly, the *Qahal*, to enter into His trinitarian community. He called His Chosen People, the Israelites (Ex 3:9-10) out of the slavery of Egypt. They were in need of a *conversion*. They had to turn away from the fleshpots of Egypt to encounter Yahweh in the desert by deep faith, hope, and loving obedience (Ex 12:50). God elected them as His favored people and to them He promised His faithful, protective love (Ex 19:1-9; 34:10-27).

God solemnizes His covenant in a ritual, "signing" action (Ex 24:3-11). He gives a sign of His covenant election by the remembered sign to be commemorated on the Sabbath of each week (Ex 20:8-9).

Thus we see that in all of God's dealings with human communities He is personally involved in issuing the call to share more intimately in His very own life and being; this can come about only by our personal and communal *conversion*. Such a change of "heart" floods us with an experienced knowledge of God's *election*. God confirms His election of His People by a *covenant action* that is to be commemorated in a repeated *sign*.

The New Covenant

It is, however, in the New Testament that we, who belong to Jesus, can understand how Jesus in His resurrection, not only unveils how He is the fullness and the power and the glory of Yahweh who so intimately worked among His People in times past, but He is able to actualize God's covenant by allowing us to live in Him and to receive of His power and glory to bring others into God's family. The New Testament is a record of the faith of the first Christian community as it reflects on God's actions among His People, especially in the fulfilling actions of His Son Jesus risen in glory. We see this in the reflection of the author of the Letter to the Hebrews:

> At various times in the past and in various different ways, God spoke to our ancestors through His Son, the Son that he has appointed to inherit everything and through whom he made everything there is. He is the radiant light of God's glory and the perfect copy of his nature, sustaining the universe by his powerful command; and now that he has destroyed the defilement of sin, he has gone to take his place in heaven at the right hand of divine Majesty. So he is now as far above the angels as the title which he has inherited is higher than their own name. (Heb. 1:1-4)

Only in the light of Christ's resurrection can we understand not only the beginning of God's involving love toward mankind but also the end, the goal and final glorification. Jesus Christ, the perfect "image of the unseen God" (Col 1:15), in whom all things have been created, has been "called" by His Father to bring all things into fulfillment.

> As he is the Beginning,
> he was first to be born from the dead,
> so that he should be first in every way;
> because God wanted all perfection
> to be found in him
> and all things to be reconciled through him and for him,
> everything in heaven and everything on earth,
> when he made peace
> by his death on the cross.
>
> Col 1:18–20

Now we can understand the mystery of God's loving activities in creating a beautiful world teeming with variety and richness, complexity and harmony. Now we can comprehend our dignity for each human being has been made "little less than a god" (Ps 8:5). We can tremble with reverent awe at God's infinite love in giving us His only begotten Son.

> Yes, God loved the world so much
> that he gave his only Son,
> so that everyone who believes in him may not be lost
> but may have eternal life.
> For God sent his Son into the world
> not to condemn the world,
> but so that through him the world might be saved.
> No one who believes in him will be condemned;
> but whoever refuses to believe is condemned already,
> because he has refused to believe
> in the name of God's only Son.
>
> Jn 3:16–18

Light over Darkness

In spite of "sin which lives inside my body" (Rom 7:23) and an entire creation that has been groaning in travail in one act of giving cosmic birth to the universe (Rom 8:22), you and I, by faith in the presence of the risen Jesus, who can do all things as the Lord of the Universe, can believe and hope in His infinite power and glory.

No matter how much darkness lies within us and outside of us in the surrounding world, we can believe that "the night is over and the real light is already shining" (1 Jn 2:8). Jesus risen has conquered sin and death and now gives us a share in His paschal victory. God's great love for us was revealed when He sent into our world His only Son (1 Jn 4:9) so that we even now share in His eternal life.

Therefore, His love poured into our hearts by His Spirit (Rom 5:5) drives out of our hearts all fear. Nothing can ever separate us from His love (Rom 8:39). We are "stamped with the seal of the Holy Spirit of the Promise . . . which brings freedom for those whom God has taken for his own, to make his glory praised" (Eph 1:13–14).

To Live in Mystery

All too often we have trivialized the resurrection of Jesus (and, therefore, our own) by objectivizing it as a static moment that happened in time and space to the dead Christ and that will happen to us at the end of the world. The mystery of God's love unfolding in constant fidelity within the context of Jesus' daily growth as a human being confronted with choices toward self-surrendering love is clouded over. We habitually objectivize Jesus in static moments of His having suffered, then died, and after His soul separated from His body, it reentered it on the third day, and He left the tomb as fully risen. This is not the mystery of the resurrection but the parody of a person resuscitated.

The empty tomb, in such thinking, becomes central as the proof for all sincere persons that Jesus is truly divine, for only God can raise the dead, in this case, Himself, from the dead. We Christians can easily "handle" such a resurrection. It puts no burden upon us to accept such a God-Man. We do not have to exercise much faith to conceive of a similar resurrection when our souls will return to our bodies on the last day of the general resurrection. Above all, we do not see the resurrection of Jesus as the fulfillment of all God's intervention into human existence to share His covenant-love with us.

We isolate the single act of Jesus' resurrection from the vast horizons of God's pursuing and ever-involving love for us human beings, from the beginning of time down to this present moment and beyond to the end of human time. By approaching the resurrection as a mysterious sign of

God's culminating love, we remain in a mystery of faith that opens us up to a continued conversion of heart. Such a conversion allows God's Spirit radically to change our concepts about God and the manner in which He exercises, through the presence of the risen Jesus in our lives, our ongoing sharing in His resurrection.

This approach in mystery combines an interaction between historical evidences and God-given faith. In the words of Blaise Pascal: "We know the truth not only through our reason but also through our heart."[3] By seeking knowledge of the heart that builds upon historical evidence recorded in the New Testament, we open ourselves up to the transforming experience of the resurrection of Jesus sweeping us into a sharing in His power and glory. We begin to see that His resurrection cannot be separated from His entire human existence on this earth and His dynamic, living presence within our universe at this *now* moment of time.

By living in the fullness of the mystery of Christ's resurrection, we move easily away from an *either/or* dualism to approach prayerfully the ever now of His resurrectional presence and our personal involvement in the same process by means of *antithesis*.

Saint Luke understood the need of comprehending the whole Christ in His sufferings and death and resurrection when he wrote:

> You foolish men! So slow to believe the full message of the prophets! Was it not ordained that the Christ should suffer and so enter into his glory? Then starting with Moses and going through all the prophets, he explained to them the passages throughout the scriptures that were about himself. (Lk 24:25–27)

After Saint Peter cured the lame man at the Beautiful Gate, he spoke to the crowds that had gathered in amazement at this sudden healing:

> You are Israelites, and it is the God of Abraham, Isaac and Jacob, the God of our ancestors, who has glorified his servant Jesus, the same Jesus you handed over and then disowned in the presence of Pilate after Pilate had decided to release Him . . . you killed the prince of life, God, however, raised him from the dead, and to that fact we are the witnesses. (Acts 3:13–15)

God of History

In both of these texts we see the use of *antithetical* language to express God's mysterious workings among His chosen people of Israel, climaxing in the raising up to glory of the dead Jesus. There is always an appeal to the listeners to make a decision on behalf of this risen Jesus, a decision that would change their lives as they too are invited to experience the similar antithetical process of embracing suffering out of love to enter into the resurrectional union with the same risen Jesus.

This approach is especially noticeable in chapters 11 and 12 of the Letter to the Hebrews. Here we see the author appealing to God's mysterious working among His people by the gift of faith that alone can "prove the existence of the realities that at present remain unseen" (Heb 11:2). We are caught up in the web of God's faithful, loving commitment to intervene among His people and lead them into the fullness of life. Abel, Enoch, and Noah, Abraham and Sarah, Isaac and Jacob, Moses, Joshua, and Rahab, the kings, judges, and prophets of Israel are presented as witnesses to be imitated by us in throwing off everything that hinders the workings of God in our lives. But the long chain of "faithful" pilgrims is climaxed by the example of Jesus Christ. Not only does He give us an example of living amidst difficulties by deep faith, but because of His resurrection and exaltation at the right hand of God's throne, He intercedes through His power and glory to give us a share in His resurrection. By faith in the resurrection of Jesus, "we have been given possession of an unshakeable kingdom. Let us therefore hold on to the grace that we have been given and use it to worship God in the way that he finds acceptable in reverence and fear" (Heb 12:28).

The Paradox of the Cross

God has brought Jesus back from the dead "to become the great Shepherd of the sheep by the blood that sealed an eternal covenant" (Heb 13:20). God's involvement in the various covenants, in which historically He pledged to be faithful to His promise to protect and share His life with His chosen people, reaches its culmination in the resurrection of Jesus who fulfills all other covenants as by the outpouring of His blood He establishes a New Covenant. "This cup is the new covenant in my blood which will be poured out for you" (Lk 22:20).

Everywhere on the pages of the New Testament we find joy expressed because Jesus has suffered and died for love of His followers and has gone forward into a completely new existence which He now makes it possible for His disciples to share. "I was dead and now I am to live forever and ever, and I hold the keys of death and of the underworld" (Rev 1:18). Saint Paul shows the intimate connection between Jesus' death and resurrection and our own justification when he writes of "Jesus who was put to death for our sins and raised to life to justify us" (Rom 4:25). Jesus "died and was raised to life" (2 Cor 5:15) in order that we might have eternal life. The resurrection of Christ is not only pivotal to the life and mission of Jesus; it is fundamental to God's actions throughout all human history. That is why Saint Paul saw so clearly the centrality of Jesus' resurrection: ". . . if Christ has not been raised, you are still in your sins" (1 Cor 15:17).

The Pauline scholar, Ernst Käsemann, summarized the glory of Jesus in His resurrection as His ability to lead His disciples on earth to share in His death and resurrection process:

> For Paul the glory of Jesus consists in the fact that he makes his disciples on earth willing and capable to bear the cross after him, and the glory of the church and of Christian life consists in the fact that they have the honor of glorifying the crucified Christ as the wisdom and power of God, to seek salvation in him alone, and to let their lives become a service to God under the sign of Golgotha. The theology of the resurrection is at this point a chapter in the theology of the cross, not its supersession.[4]

Paradoxes of Christianity

Over and over in the pages of the New Testament we find antitheses, paradoxes that seek by various metaphors or symbols to express the mystery of God's in-breaking love in order to share with us His very own life. Jesus preached about death-life, darkness-light, bondage-freedom. But above all, He came among human beings and lived such paradoxes. He was the light that came into the darkness, even though the darkness did not comprehend Him (Jn 1:9–11). He came to bring life, and that more abundantly, to those who were sick and dying (Jn 10:10). He was the power in whom all things were created and made (Jn 1:2; Col 1:16), yet He appeared in weakness, crucified and emptied out on the cross for love of us. In His humiliations He was lifted up (Jn 12:32) and exalted in glory by His Father (Phil 2:10). He descended into our world, tempted in all things, save sin (Heb 4:15) in order that we might ascend with Him into heavenly glory (Eph 4:8–10). His defeat on the cross by the powers of evil led to eternal victory over sin and death. His shame turned to glory and He holds out to us the same possibility of suffering with Him in order that we might also enter into glory with Him (Rom 8:17).

He was the second Adam who offset the fall of the first Adam and He now makes it possible for us to put off the old self and put on the new man (Eph 4:22; 2 Cor 5:18). Through His resurrectional life living in us through the release of His Spirit, we can become "spiritual" persons (Rom 8:9–11) by putting off the perishable and the corruptible and by living as already in the incorruptible life of the Spirit. He has destroyed sin and death and has restored us to become children of the Heavenly Father (Rom 8:16; Gal 4:6). We have been baptized into His death and He has raised us to new life. He has gone away from this earth and yet He remains always with us, as He and the Father come and abide within us to share their trinitarian life with us.

To live in the mystery of Jesus' resurrection is to allow His victory to exercise daily a transforming power in our lives. This victory is the experienced knowledge of the Father and Jesus, His Son, through the Holy Spirit, in their infinite love always being poured out into our hearts (Rom 5:5). It is this knowledge that brings eternal life and a share even now in the victory of His resurrection (Jn 17:3). This knowledge, received in prayer, is experienced freshly every time you and I live in self-sacrificing love for another person. Only in such a manner can we experientially know the infinite love of God in Jesus, that drove Him in dying for us to empty Himself unto the last drop of blood as He imaged on the cross the perfect love of the Heavenly Father for us.

We need to turn lovingly to this mystery that surpasses all our own human, finite knowledge (Eph 3:17–18) in order to transcend the limitations of our concepts of time and space and to pass into the experience of resurrectional time and space. Christ by His resurrection has conquered the limitations imposed upon time and space by our sinful condition and, through the release of His Spirit within our hearts, we are able to live on a new level of consciousness that explodes time and space into an exciting, ever *now* moment, the *kairos* time of salvation. In this new time, in our brokenness of each moment, we are able to meet the living-giving healing love of Jesus. The risen and exalted Jesus sweeps us into a sharing in His power and glory that knows none of the limitations of ordinary time and space. Let us turn to the *new time* that Jesus brought into being by His resurrection and that He shares with us through His Spirit so that we too can even now live in His victory over all limitations.

NOTES

1. W.H. Auden, from "For the Time Being," in *The Collected Poetry*, ed. Edward Mendelson (New York: Random House, 1945), p. 447.

2. Alexander Solzhenitsyn, *The Gulag Archipelago, 1918–1956: An Experiment in Literary Investigation*, vol. 2, trans. Thomas P. Whitney, (New York: Harper & Row, 1975), p. 615.

3. Blaise Pascal, *Les Pensées*, 110.

4. Ernst Käsemann, "The Pauline Theology of the Cross," in *Interpretation* 24, no. 2, p. 177; cited by Lloyd Geering, *Resurrection: A Symbol of Hope* (London: Hodder and Stoughton, 1971), p. 225.

Chapter Two

NEW TIME AND NEW SPACE

Love has the unique power to catch up space and time and transform them into an experience of two persons becoming one in spacelessness that knows no harshness of ticking time. In love you burst the limitations of confining space. You soar through the firmaments of past, present, and future as you learn to rest in the ever-abiding *now* moment of loving union. No place can hold you within its painful grasp as you stretch to touch the ecstasy of eternity.

Saint John of the Cross explains how love transcends the limits of our earthly bodies. "The soul lives where it loves rather than in the body which it animates, because it has not its life in the body, but rather gives it to the body and lives through love in that which it loves."[1]

We have all experienced in love what the English Jesuit poet Robert Southwell wrote: "Not where I breathe do I live but where I love." By the death and resurrection of Jesus Christ, we can now receive His same Holy Spirit of love who brought the risen Lord into a new existence that destroyed the boundaries and limitations of time and space.

While on this earth Jesus of Nazareth, in His humanity, submitted Himself to the weaknesses and infirmities of a human being immersed in the collective sinfulness and death that color every human being's experience of brokenness in time and space. In a place and in a given time Jesus underwent struggles and temptations in all things as we do, yet He did not sin (Heb 4:15). As He inched His way through each moment of His earthly existence up to His final hour on the cross, Jesus surrendered increasingly to the Father's infinite love for Him.

His human soul received the fullness of the Father's Spirit at the moment when He "passed over" the limits of earthly time and space and entered into a new age.

The Last Age

In the death of Jesus on the cross God the Father thundered out His everlasting No to sin and death. He smilingly whispered at the same time His Yes to the new age. In Jesus the Last Day that could never be held within the broken limitations of earthly space and time had dawned and would never see a setting.

The resurrection of Christ is a new beginning which brings to an end the domination of historical time and space. And yet His resurrection happens within the orbit of earthly time and space. God mysteriously has now entered into the history of humanity and from inside is setting about to destroy sin, corruption, and death. This is done completely in Jesus, but gradually through His risen presence living in His living members who become His leaven, God speaks to raise all of humanity into a sharing of Jesus' new life.

A.M. Ramsey clearly shows that the resurrection is "not merely a great event upon the plane of history, but an act that breaks into history with the powers of another world. It is akin to the creation in the beginning; and the Gospel is the good news that God is creating a new world."[2]

Sharing His Resurrection

All God's creative power becomes completely concentrated in the person of the risen Jesus. Saint Paul writes: "He was crucified through weakness, yet he lives by the power of God" (2 Cor 13:4). God fills His humanity with the fullness of His power and glory. "He was established Son of God in power by the resurrection of the dead" (Rom 1:4).

Because Jesus risen now possesses in His humanity the fullness of the Father's Spirit, we human beings can now receive of Jesus' Spirit. Jesus, by His resurrection, is now the "Prince of life" (Acts 3:15). He is now the cause, origin, center, and goal of the entire world.

> As he is the Beginning,
> he was first to be born from the dead,
> so that he should be first in every way;
> because God wanted all perfection
> to be found in him
> and all things to be reconciled through him and for him,
> everything in heaven and everything on earth,

when he made peace
by his death on the cross.

Col 1:18–20

Jesus, the Pantocrator of the universe, makes it possible now for us to share in His resurrection. It means that we can be risen only insofar as we are united with the risen Lord and share in the one resurrection, which is that of Jesus. The Father raises up only His Son. There is only His resurrection. We shall not be raised up individually and separated from Jesus' single resurrection.

F.X. Durrwell rather forcefully points out the singleness of our resurrection with that of Jesus:

> This plan (God's saving plan) is put into execution with Christ's resurrection. The action whereby the body of the mortal Christ is transformed inaugurates the Father's action of justification; divine life comes to mortal man; the justice of God, which is a living and life-giving holiness, takes possession of him. It is the Father who raises up Christ (Rom 8:11; 1 Cor 6:14; 2 Cor 4:15; 13:4; Eph 1:19; Col 2:12) and who justifies us (Rom 3:26, 30; 8:30; Gal 3:8). It is in Christ, and through the act of raising him up, that he justifies us. The resurrection of our Lord is the first of the Father's life-giving works in a new world, the first and only one, for all the others are accomplished in it: "He has quickened us together with Christ" (Eph 2:5).[3]

Our Resurrection Already Now

Saint Paul, only at the end of his earthly life, evolved in the letters to the Ephesians and Colossians his teaching that even in this life we too share in Christ's resurrection. In Baptism we Christians are buried with Christ and "by baptism, too, you have been raised up with him through your belief in the power of God who raised him from the dead" (Col 2:12). By taking away our sins and bringing us to life with Christ, God "raised us up with him and gave us a place with him in heaven, in Christ Jesus" (Eph 2:5–6).

This new life in Christ is already yours in Baptism and grows each time you "put on Christ" by dying to selfishness and rising to a new oneness in Him. This new life is "not yet" in its fullness. Your bodily life, your total personhood, is still in the process of being baptized at each moment in Christ. This life is hidden with Christ in God and will only appear with the manifestation of the fullness of Christ in God in His *Pa-*

rousia (second coming). Saint Paul's understanding of the resurrection had been earlier oriented to the future end of the world, but toward the end of his life it became increasingly an experience in Christ that has already begun and is to increase as we cooperate to allow His new time and space to operate in our lives.[4]

We through Baptism and Eucharist form one Body with the Risen Christ. Jesus is the principle of our life in Him, but He is such through His new resurrectional life. This is a new life which Jesus did not possess earlier in His bodily humanity. And this new life He shares already now with us who live in Him. We enter into eternal life by sharing the Spirit of Jesus. "But anyone who is joined to the Lord is one spirit with him" (1 Cor 6:17).This participation admits of various degrees of intensity and growth, depending on our readiness to die to self-centeredness and rise to the new life in Jesus. "And we, with our unveiled faces reflecting like mirrors the brightness of the Lord, all grow brighter and brighter as we are turned into the image that we reflect; this is the work of the Lord who is Spirit" (2 Cor 3:18).

Ever Younger

Jesus by His resurrection undoes in His own Person and in our lives as well what Adam, the first parent of the human race, did by his sin. Jesus enters into a new birth by His resurrection. The signs of the time and space into which Adam and his progeny were immersed are death and corruption. The signs of the New Adam are an ever growing youthfulness and increase in life and beauty and happiness.

He who was eternally one with God (Phil 2:6) came into a new birth at Easter. He "was proclaimed Son of God in all his power through his resurrection from the dead" (Rom 1:4). Saint Paul boldly applies Psalm 2:7 to Jesus' new birth as God's Son in the resurrection.

> We have come here to tell you the Good News. It was to our ancestors that God made the promise but it is to us, their children, that he has fulfilled it, by raising Jesus from the dead. As scripture says in the first psalm: You are my son: today I have become your father. The fact that God raised him from the dead, never to return to corruption, is no more than what he had declared: To you I shall give the sure and holy things promised to David. This is explained by another text: You will not allow your holy one to experience corruption. Now when David in his own time had served God's purposes he

died; he was buried with his ancestors and has certainly experienced corruption. The one whom God has raised up, however has not experienced corruption. (Acts 13:32–37)

Time is reversed as Jesus, through His resurrection, is eternally being begotten. Christmas is caught forever in the Easter event. Jesus Christ can no longer grow older nor can He be subjected to corruption and death. He is being renewed daily in glory and power. His dominion extends to all nations and to all parts of the world.

The first Christian community stammers and stutters as individual teachers reflect on this "new creation" and the excitement they felt as they encountered the "New Man" in a new and ever-fresh life.

When I saw him, I fell in a dead faint at his feet, but he touched me with his right hand and said, 'Do not be afraid; it is I, *the First* and *the Last*; I am the Living One, I was dead and now I am to live for ever and ever, and I hold the keys of death and of the underworld. (Rev 1:17–18)

Time has been redeemed. The past times and places have been healed of their limitations and brokenness. And now time and space have been carried forward into the future but a future of ever-increasing life and happiness.

A Youthful Church

This new creation, in a new time and an endless space to extend over all the universe, Jesus shares with His followers, the members of His one Body, His Church. As we give up our "old" ways of life, as Saint Paul teaches (Eph 4:22), by putting aside our old selves that have been corrupted by our following illusory desires, we are to renew our minds by a spiritual revolution, "so that you can put on the new self that has been created in God's way, in the goodness and holiness of the truth" (Eph 4:24).

We are no longer children of darkness but of the light, a new creation by being in Jesus Christ (2 Cor 5:17). We are to fashion ourselves as a beautiful, virginal bride to be given to Christ in glory, "with no speck or wrinkle or anything like that, but holy and faultless" (Eph 5:27).

The Shepherd of Hermas, in his five visions of the Church written in the early part of the second century, portrays the Church first as an old woman because she was created the first of all things since for her the world was built.[5] But the powerful insight that Hermas passes on to us is that that Church is also eternally young, becoming younger and younger as she lives in the life of the risen Christ. She is the *ecclesia neotera*, the "younger and younger Church," yet she is still seen as a woman with white hair to show that, although she is ever new and young, she is also older than the world and in relationship to the historical world and made up of the elements of that "old" world.

The Millenium

We who are in Christ already have entered into the millenium, the apocalyptic term to describe an endless time of blissful perfection and fulfillment. We stretch forth to Christ's return in full glory as we longingly cry out "Maran atha," "the Lord is coming" (1Cor 16:22). Yet we rejoice that God has broken into our historical time and space by Jesus' resurrection and the *New Jerusalem* is already given to us. God is already among us making all things new in the risen Jesus.

> Then I saw *a new heaven and a new earth*; the first heaven and the first earth had disappeared now, and there was no longer any sea. I saw the holy city, and the new Jerusalem, coming down from God out of heaven, as beautiful as a bride all dressed for her husband. Then I heard a loud voice call from the throne. You see this city? Here God lives among men. He will make *his home among them; they shall be his people*, and he will be their God; his name is *God-with-them. He will wipe away all tears from their eyes*; there will be no more death, and no more mourning or sadness. The world of the past has gone. (Rev 21:1-4)

Satan is already bound for these "thousand years" (Rev 20:2). He has lost all power over those who belong to Christ. We, who wish to put on Christ and live in Him, bringing every thought and imagination in obedience and submission to Him (2 Cor 10:5), are destined while we live on this earth to live in the tension of the "already" and the "not yet." Christ, by His resurrection and the life He shares with us in His Church, has conquered fragmented historical time and space. He is always here, not coming. He is always conquering sin and death in our lives. And yet we still journey in earthly time and space. Our bodily death will end for us our immersion in time and place and we shall enter into a new manifestation of the glorious coming of Christ to lead us into eternal life that will never be subjected to corruption and death.

In Christ

Until He comes in the fullness of the Last Day, for us at our bodily death and for the world at the final day of its consummation, we struggle in faith, hope, and love to receive more fully in this *now* moment of salvation a share of His life. But we need to live already in the victory that the risen Jesus has won for Himself and that He wishes to share with us.

We are not to ignore the time in which we now find ourselves struggling to surrender to the New Adam and the New Age. We cannot leap over the place that situates us in God's plan of salvation no matter how confining and restrictive that space may seem to be. The world around us and the worldly, demonic elements even within us are to provide for us the time and space in which we can experience a sharing in the death-resurrection of Jesus.

Our constant prayer should be that of Saint Paul:

> All I want is to know Christ and the power of his resurrection and to share his sufferings by reproducing the pattern of his death. That is the way I can hope to take my place in the resurrection of the dead. Not that I have the prize for which Christ Jesus captured me. I can assure you, my brothers, I am far from thinking that I have already won. All I can say is that I forget the past and I strain ahead for what is still to come; I am racing for the finish, for the prize to which God calls us upwards to receive in Christ Jesus. We who are called 'perfect' must all think in this way . . . meanwhile let us go forward on the road that has brought us to where we are. (Phil 3:10–16)

Amid the filth and sordidness of a broken world that spreads its menacing tentacles around us on all sides and at every moment, we believe that the risen Lord is in-breaking into our world and is bringing us His healing love and a share already in His everlasting life. The power of the risen Jesus is greater than any outside force and that power is living within us! ". . . you are from God and you have in you one who is greater than anyone in this world" (1 Jn 4:4).

We, as Christians, breathe already the paschal victory of Christ, even as we are surrounded by the powers of darkness. With Saint Paul we, too, can shout out our hope in the risen Jesus to come to our rescue.

> Nothing therefore can come between us and the love of Christ, even
> if we are troubled or worried, or being persecuted, or lacking food or

clothes, or being threatened or even attacked. As scripture promised: For your sake we are being massacred daily, and reckoned as sheep for the slaughter. These are the trials through which we triumph, by the power of him who loved us. For I am certain of this: neither death nor life, no angel, no prince, nothing that exists, nothing still to come, not any power, or height or depth, nor any created thing can ever come between us and the love of God made visible in Christ Jesus our Lord. (Rom 8:35–39)

Transformation

Our present time and space, by the presence of the risen Lord and our cooperation with Him and His Spirit, have no longer a negative power over us. But more positively our faith, hope and love for the risen Lord lead us to a new framework in which we are called to bring the transforming power of Christ's new life into our very time and space. Having experienced the healing love of the risen Jesus, living within us and abiding there with His eternal Father through His Spirit of love, we are empowered to take our broken moment in the history of the human race and our place in that disjointed history in order to transform them into a new age.

We are called to be Christ's ambassadors and reconcilers of this shattered world (2 Cor 5:17–20) to bring all things to God. The old time and space are still with us and we journey in them along with the broken ones of this world. Yet the Good News is that Jesus is risen and is bringing through us His power and glory to uplift and transform this tired and dying world into the *New Creation*, that is to become the total Christ.

This Christ is now in pilgrimage through a dark and arid desert. His Body in time and space is broken but it is constantly being healed by the Spirit's love. He, who said, "I am the resurrection and the life. If anyone believes in me, even though he dies he will live, and whoever lives and believes in me will never die" (Jn 11:25–26), has not left us to struggle alone. He is with us and we already live in His power and glory.

We can summarize this chapter by reflecting prayerfully on the Gospel account of Jesus as He healed the paralytic presented to Him through the roof of the house where Jesus was preaching. He raises the paralytic from his stretcher and both forgives him his sins and heals him of his paralysis (Mk 2:1–12; Lk 5:17–26). Jesus risen is here among us now preaching and bringing healing within the context of our broken time and space. A paralytic is lifted down to Christ through his faith, a gift

from above, to touch Him and to receive a share in His new life that
overcomes all evils of body, soul and spirit. The resurrection of Jesus is to
be not merely a historical event that happened to Him at Easter. Jesus is
raising up the broken ones of this world by being inserted still into their
world of suffering in time and space.

The Spirit of Love

Jesus in His resurrectional presence is close to us in the very context of
our disjointed time and space. He is ready to release His Spirit who allowed Him in His humanity to transcend the limitations of human, historical time and space. This same Spirit convinces us that the Heavenly
Father, who has loved us with an everlasting love, loves us in His perfectly fulfilled word-made-flesh, Jesus Christ.

We are the people "who were once brought into the light, and tasted
the gift from heaven, and received a share of the Holy Spirit, and appre-
ciated the good message of God and the powers of the world to come"
(Heb 6:4–5). We are humbled in believing that those powers of the
world to come are already given to us in this vale of tears by Jesus risen.
"All authority in heaven and on earth has been given to me. Go, therefore, make disciples of all nations. . . . And know that I am with you
always; yes, to the end of time" (Mt 28:18–20).

We belong to the Victor who has conquered sin, death, and all the
limitations of time and space that Saint Paul lumps together in the one
word, *corruption*. All our actions we seek to perform in His name, in return for His eternal love for us. His power, wisdom, grace, strength, in a
word His Spirit becomes our sharing in Jesus' resurrection.

Time and space hold us in their grasp, but now we know that we live
in Christ and, therefore, even now we live forever. God's love for us and
His entire world casts out all fear from our hearts as we remain in a broken world, but no longer broken by our place and time in God's drama
to bring all things into completion. Saint Paul shows us how we are to
live already now in the risen Jesus as we die to our self-centeredness, to
our "worldliness," and live in His Spirit's love.

> Since you have been brought back to true life with Christ, you must
> look for the things that are in heaven, where Christ is, sitting at
> God's right hand. Let your thoughts be on heavenly things, not on
> the things that are on the earth, because you have died, and now the
> life you have is hidden with Christ in God. But when Christ is re-

vealed—and he is your life—you too will be revealed in all your glory with him. (Col 3:1–4)

NOTES

1. Saint John of the Cross, *The Spiritual Canticle*, in *The Collected Works of Saint John of the Cross*, trans. Kieran Kavanaugh, O.C.D., and Otilio Rodriguez, O.C.D. (Washington, D.C.: Institute of Carmelite Studies, 1973), p. 441.

2. A. M. Ramsey, *The Resurrection of Christ* (London: G. Bles, 1945), p. 31.

3. F. X. Durrwell, *The Resurrection: A Biblical Study*, 2nd ed., trans. Rosemary Sheed (New York: Sheed and Ward, 1960), p. 32.

4. On this point, see Pierre Benoit, O.P., "Resurrection: At the End of Time or Immediately After Death?" in *Immortality and Resurrection*, vol. 60 of *Concilium* (New York: Herder and Herder, 1970), pp. 103–14.

5. *The Shepherd of Hermas*, Vision 2, 4, 1.

6. Vision 2, 10.

Chapter Three

A LIGHT THAT SHINES
IN THE DARK

The Byzantine icon of the resurrection is never an objectivized picture of the historical Jesus coming out of the tomb; rather, Jesus is depicted as pulling an aged man out of the bowels of the earth. It is an artistic commentary on the Christian theological truth that Jesus, by His resurrection, entered into the hellish areas of human existence and there destroyed death and sin. Usually this icon portrays Christ stepping over the doors of hell with the instruments of His passion scattered about. He pulls Adam out of the underworld, while Hades is personified as a demon trying to hold him back.[1]

Resurrection is a new age as God *now* is restoring the human race to a new life in Christ. A new creation, not only of the risen Jesus, but of human beings sharing in His new life and the whole cosmos transfigured by His glorious presence, has begun.

Jesus in this icon is acting out the words of the Book of Revelation: "I was dead and now I am to live forever and ever, and I hold the keys of death and of the underworld" (1:18). Jesus "died and was raised to life" (2 Cor 5:15) for us that we might have eternal life. Saint Peter gives to succeeding generations of Christians the insight into the mystery of Jesus conquering sin and death when he writes:

> In the body he was put to death, in the spirit he was raised to life, and, in the spirit, he went to preach to the spirits in prison. . . . And because he is their judge too, the dead had to be told the Good News as well, so that though, in their life on earth, they had been through the judgment that comes to all humanity, they might come to God's life in the spirit. (1 Pet 3:19–4:6)

Jesus risen is still a Light that shines in the darkness of sin and death that inhabit all of us and through us cover the entire cosmos with their black cloud of non-being. This is beautifully enacted in the Byzantine churches in the midnight Easter service as the priests and deacons and the entire congregation with lighted candles march out of the church, leaving it in darkness. The main celebrant from outside the closed doors knocks and then begins to sing with joyful triumph: "Christ is risen from the dead, trampling down death by death, and granting life to those in the tomb!" He and the congregation enter into the dark church with lighted candles as they literally shout out the refrain: "Christ is risen! He is truly risen!" In such a communal experience it becomes somewhat easier to believe that Jesus the Light is still among us, divinizing us by pouring out upon us His loving Spirit who can dispell all sin and darkness.

Jesus, the Healing Light

Historically Jesus entered into our dark world. He truly was "a light that shines in the dark, a light that darkness could not overpower" (Jn 1:4–5). Within Himself He fought the darkness of temptations. He knew the fears that impending death could bring Him as He begged His heavenly Father to remove the cup of suffering from Him (Lk 22:42). Above all, He confronted the powers of evil darkness that held the bodies, souls and spirits of human beings in bondage. He drove out demons and cured the sick and the diseased. He came to set all human beings free from their captivity.

> He has sent me to bring the good news to the poor,
> to proclaim liberty to captives
> and to the blind new sight
> to set the downtrodden free,
> to proclaim the Lord's year of favour.
>
> Lk 4:18

As Jesus entered into the darkness within the daily lives of those whom He met on this earth and led them into the light of His healing love, so He is able to meet us in our darkened sufferings and heal us also.

The Paschal Victory

Through His resurrection Jesus Christ is able to touch our crippling fears and petty slaveries and lead us out into true freedom. It is His

Spirit, who alone can lead us in a prayerful encountering with the risen Jesus "to know Christ and the power of His resurrection and to share His sufferings by reproducing the pattern of his death. That is the way I can hope to take my place in the resurrection of the dead" (Phil 3:10–12). We are free to the degree that we desire to surrender to the Spirit of Jesus to take away all our fears and transfigure our sufferings into life-giving love. Even now we are able to live in the freeing power of the risen Lord.

With Saint Paul, we can boast of our own weakness (2 Cor 11:30) for our total strength is in Jesus Christ: " . . . and by God's doing He has become our wisdom, and our virtue, and our holiness, and our *freedom*" (1 Cor 1:30). We are free because "we are those who have the mind of Christ" (1 Cor 2:16).

The risen Lord can conquer in our lives by the revelation of His Spirit. We can be freed from sin and death and the false values of the world and live in the freedom of the risen people of God. The brokenness and sufferings that we find at every turn of our daily lives can be turned from death-dealing to life-giving opportunities as we allow Jesus to lead us into such freedom. Saint Paul describes how he and his fellow Christians turned all sufferings and persecutions into a new sharing in the resurrection of Jesus:

> Here we are, fools for the sake of Christ, while you are the learned men in Christ; we have no power, but you are influential; you are celebrities, we are nobodies. To this day, we go without food and drink and clothes; we are beaten and have no homes; we work for our living with our own hands. When we are cursed, we answer with a blessing; when we are hounded, we put up with it; we are insulted and we answer politely. We are treated as the offal of the world, still to this day, the scum of the earth. (1 Cor 4:10–13)

Jesus is Victor over death and all sufferings. He conquers our hearts as He, the living Word of God, speaks from within us of His eternal love that images the love of the Father for us. Freedom is no longer the ability to choose between good and evil; it is the progressive surrender in love to Him so that in each moment we live for Him, our Lord. He is the inner force that allows us to catch any given moment of our history with all its brokenness, filth, confining meaninglessness and raise it unto the level of God's *eternal now*. His Spirit brings us into an ever-growing awareness of our true dignity before the world. In that dignity of being loved infinitely by God in Christ Jesus, we are free to love as He loves us. Freedom, as God gives us this great gift in Jesus risen, is nothing less than the gift of loving ourselves and the entire world as God loves us and with God's love in us.

Suffering

From the Synoptic Gospels we see that Jesus taught three essential elements about Himself: He announced the in-breaking of the Kingdom of God among men; this in-breaking would be tied intrinsically to His own suffering and death; and lastly, He would rise triumphantly from the dead and pour out His Spirit to share His new power and glory with all His followers. He taught this fundamental law of human growth in many ways. Over and over again He insisted that, if His disciples wished to have a share in His life, "to have a part of Me," then they would have to deny themselves and take up their crosses and follow Him (Mt 16:24–25; Mk 8:34–35; Lk 9:23–24). It was only by losing one's life for His sake that a person would truly find it.

Jesus taught death-resurrection, hatred toward one's false self in order to love oneself truly in Christ, when He preached:

> I tell you, most solemnly,
> unless a wheat grain falls on the ground and dies,
> it remains only a single grain;
> but if it dies,
> it yields a rich harvest.
> Anyone who loves his life loses it;
> anyone who hates his life in this world
> will keep it for the eternal life.
>
> Jn 12:24–25

But Jesus lived out this law of suffering unto greater life. The Gospel accounts of His earthly life present it in terms of the *Exodus*. He was passing over from death unto life everlasting. He was constantly tempted to yield to His death-dealing, fearful side of His being, to presume on the love of His Father, to demand in pride that He be recognized by worldly power as the Son of God. In the agony in the garden He confronted the fears that could have been an obstacle to His rising to new heights of love toward His Father and toward every human being for whom He would suffer. He did not want to die. In His agony He sweated blood.

The Spirit of love was challenging Him to enter into the dark side within Him, into the collective consciousness of the fears of the entire human race that would seek power, rather than the weakness of suffering love.

As in the garden of Gethsemane, so on the cross, Jesus struggled to do battle within Himself to submit completely in obedience to His Father. The Greek Fathers were fond of calling the Savior of the world, the *sperma logikon*, the Logos Seed of Divine Life, that was inserted into our suffering and sinful humanity. The soldiers on Calvary lifted that Divine Seed aloft and then plunged it into the hole prepared for it in the earth. Its whole side was split and at the very moment that the Seed seemed to have perished, an inner life burst forth into a new and glorious eternal life. Jesus was risen on Calvary! His sufferings and final death brought Him into a new life-giving power. He was glorified by the Father in that moment when He cried out triumphantly and joyfully: "Father, into your hands I commit my spirit" (Lk 23:46).

Our Sufferings

Suffering will be the lot of all of us. Whether we accept it or not, we shall still have to bear a great deal of suffering. As Job found out, suffering will always remain a mystery to our puny reasoning powers. But Jesus Christ came to give to His followers a vision of faith and the strength of His Spirit through His indwelling life, so that we too could share "his sufferings so as to share his glory" (Rom 8:17).

We suffer passively in the mere act of growing from infancy to childhood, from being a youth to reaching the full maturity of adulthood. There are biological, psychological, and spiritual sufferings that "happen" to us and are necessary if we are to grow more fully on the levels of body, soul, and spirit relationships. There will be the sufferings of sickness, the bunglings of ourselves and of others acting upon us, the doubts, fears, and anxieties from our own creatureliness and sinfulness, to our inability to cope with the many problems of life. Ultimately there will be the greatest diminishment by death itself to lead us into the final, physical suffering before we pass into eternal life.

There will be sufferings on a more active level of working in the sweat of our brow for our daily bread. This will entail much discipline and above all much monotony. It calls for a usual, banal routine that in the ultimate analysis cuts away at our egoism as we learn to transcend the momentarily monotonous into the larger vision of creative labor.

Perhaps for most of us the greatest call to suffering comes from what apparently should be the most beautiful experience of our human lives: from human love. We grow most as human beings when we are called out by another human person so forget and surrender ourselves for that person in true, self-sacrificing love. Love is an invitation to suffer. Yet how we fear to accept it. It means to say "yes" to another being, and entailed in this acceptance to love is a "no" to any conflicting selfishness.

Life-giving Suffering

Our sufferings have no intrinsic value in themselves. The very same suffering may bring more crippling fear and destructive death to ourselves, or it may bring us into a new sharing in the resurrection of Christ. Above all, we must not yield to the death-dealing belief that we deserve to suffer, that God punishes us by sending us sufferings, because we have sinned. Seeing Jesus dying on the cross as the focus of God's wrath, we prepare ourselves for greater sufferings if we believe God hates us in our sins.

In His journey on earth Jesus met the Father working at every moment, even in the sufferings that came to Him from outside agents (Jn 5:17). And He worked also in freely accepting the sufferings, irrespective of their causes, turning them into opportunities to develop His full human nature. In His humanity Jesus became the expressed Word of God by grappling, as Jacob did with the stranger (Gen 32:26), with the circumstances in which He found Himself.

He freely chose actively to accept those sufferings, and death itself, out of love for His Father and for all of us.

> The Father loves me,
> because I lay down my life
> in order to take it up again.
> No one takes it from me;
> I lay it down of my own free will,
> and as it is in my power to lay it down,
> so it is in my power to take it up again;
> and this is the command I have been given by my Father.
>
> Jn 10:17–18

So we are faced daily, in the most ordinary circumstances of our lives, with sufferings that can challenge us into greatness by transcending our own locked-in self-hatred and fear and by entering into a new, loving energy that lives for someone beyond ourselves. We think of the heroic struggle of a Helen Keller to conquer her natural handicaps in order to rise to a life that opened up to a world of beauty in her self-forgetting.

Beethoven began to lose his hearing at the age of thirty and yet in total deafness he composed for the last eighteen years of his life, producing his masterpiece, the Ninth Symphony, his *Missa Solemnis*, and many other of his greatest works. He did not withdraw into isolation and bitter hate toward his cruel fate but rose to become an even greater, creative genius. Not in spite of his deafness, but in that very deafness he pushed himself to hear new and more beautiful music, unheard before by human ear.

He came close to suicide; yet he struggled until he experienced a miracle of inner healing. He could finally write: "You will see me as happy as my lot can be here below. Not unhappy, no. That I could never endure. I will seize fate by the throat. It shall never wholly overcome me. How beautiful life is." [2]

Hope of What Could Be

Sufferings, when they are faced and accepted in the hope that something better will come from them, can help us turn within and release hidden powers that would otherwise lie fallow forever. Saint Paul brought to all his sufferings the ringing faith-vision that allowed him to bear all things unto a greater release of life. He wrote about his belief: "We know that by turning everything to their good God co-operates with all those who love him, with all those that he has called according to his purpose" (Rom 8:28).

If we learn to accept the sufferings and the many manifestations of brokenness that have made us what we are in our history, we can meet the indwelling Word of God in those very sufferings. That Word of God pours out into our hearts the Spirit of love who fills us with hope of what yet could be and, with God's power, could do infinitely more than anything we could imagine. Hope breathes the element of the impossible. Desire is a mere projection of what we think out of our present experience is still possible. Hope means concretely that anything is possible in a miracle of God's doing that far exceeds anything we could do through our own powers or even imagine.

We thus can hope that no matter how much brokenness we have inherited from our parents and their ancestors, from our evil society and its social institutions, from the persons who have acted directly upon us and left us smoldering in the ashes of fears and rejections, there can be a healing. We can experience through hope a sharing in the resurrection of Jesus.

Gabriel Marcel holds out that hope to all of us: "I can be led to recognize that deep down in me there is something other than me, something further within me than I am myself."[3] Shakespeare believed that man could be master of his fate, sometimes. The Christian, believing in the presence of the risen Lord, dwelling within him, claims through hope in Jesus Christ that he can do all things in Him who strengthens him. Amidst Saint Paul's great sufferings endured in preaching the Word of God, he describes this hope beautifully:

> We are only the earthenware jars that hold this treasure, to make it clear that such an overwhelming power comes from God and not from us. We are in difficulties on all sides, but never cornered; we see no answer to our problems, but never despair; we have been persecuted, but never deserted; knocked down, but never killed; always, wherever we may be, we carry with us in our body the death of Jesus, so that the life of Jesus, too, may always be seen in our body. Indeed, while we are still alive, we are consigned to our death every day, for the sake of Jesus, so that in our mortal flesh the life of Jesus, too, may be openly shown. So death is at work in us, but life in you. (2 Cor 4:7–12)

The Inner Battle

The risen Jesus, however, will not do it all for us. Our belief in Him as the life and resurrection (Jn 11:25–26) demands that we engage ourselves actively in the death-resurrection process through our sufferings. The sufferings we have to endure call forth the dormant powers that lie within us untapped forever, if conflicts were not to arise and lead us out of illusion into a struggle to "find" our true selves rising above the false self created in us by outside forces.

Again Marcel clearly suggests our role in the struggle: "Ours is a being whose concrete essence is to be in every way *involved* and therefore to find itself at grips with a fate which it must not only undergo, but also make its own by somehow recreating it from within."[4]

Most of us fear encountering ourselves in the depths of our being. We seek to be "on top," in charge of our lives, fearing always to let go of the false power that creates the illusion that we are what we do. Paul Tillich writes in his book *The Courage to Be*: "Actualization of being implies the ability to take courageously upon oneself the anxiety of nonbeing."[5] Shall we stay inside ourselves, in the tomb where death to the false self will lead to a new self in the Word of God? One of the great paradoxes of human existence is the fear that we have of letting go of the person we think we are, the often illusory self that society around us created and gave our name. Yet the more we hold on to the false self, the more we suffer in our self-hatred and in our isolation from living in harmony with God and our neighbor and the entire, created world.

By staying "inside" and exploring ourselves on deeper levels than we usually seek, we begin to develop a distaste for our false self. We truly learn that to hate ourselves on that level is to prepare ourselves for true love for ourselves. And only such true love for ourselves can lead us to true love for God and neighbor. As we learn to silence the noise and ploys we have been using to put off our true growth, we discover the many shams and deceits we have been employing in order to put off accepting the call to new life. We see the false posturing and the little tricks we use to push ourselves forward before others, to impress them with our worth by displaying the things we have done. We have put off finding our true identity in God's Word according to whom we have been created.

The working of God's grace to instill anxiety, fear, and disgust into us as we confront our existence in the light of our "nonbeing" is not merely a self-centered reflection on death; it is an ontological "nostalgia" to leave the "husks of swine" and return to our true selves. It is to be in love with our heavenly Father in total self-surrendering.

Dr. Carl Jung expresses the same truth in modern psychological terms:

> Only the man who is able *consciously* to affirm the power of the vocation confronting him becomes a personality; he who succumbs to it falls a prey to the blind flux of happening and is destroyed. The greatness and liberating effect of all genuine personality consists in this, that it subjects itself of free choice to its vocation and consciously translates into its own individual reality what would lead only to ruin if it were lived unconsciously.[6]

Coming to Be

Sufferings from our past, therefore, have no importance except insofar as they become an occasion to enter into true poverty by confronting the dark shadows of our inner world and exorcising them, the unreal demons, that rear their shadowy, threatening fears. H.A. Williams, an Anglican priest, describes the practice of exorcism among the Nichiren sect of Buddhism in Japan. The "possessed" person is brought to a state in which the possessing entity can speak through the patient's mouth and give its name and state the reason why it attacks the patient. After a dialogue between the exorcist and the spirit, the exorcist begins to bargain with the spirit, asking him what he wants as a price for leaving the patient. Usually the answer is: "A little shrine set up to it and an offering made to it every day." If this is done, the spirit will become a protection for the patient instead of one that inflicts harm.[7]

The demonic forces that lie embedded within the matrix of our unconscious, stored up over all our own personal experiences of the past and those of our ancestors, can never really be driven out from us. They are a part of us. They have fashioned us into the person we now are. A true exorcism can only be the acceptance of who or what we are and the assimilation of all that into a "new creation." This cannot happen without great suffering and the hope in a loving power that brings into this very suffering a joyful stretching through the suffering into new, vibrant powers never experienced before. It is not unlike the beautiful butterfly as it painfully stretches out of the confining cocoon.

Suffering in this sense does not lead to new life. It is the midwife, the medium that brings forth new life. This power of transforming suffering into joy explains the burning desire of the early martyrs who eagerly went forth to suffer unto death for the joy of being born into Christ and of sharing through that very suffering an eternal life that could never be taken from them. Simone Weil beautifully captures this paradox of death-dealing suffering that is transformed into life-giving joy:

> The joy of Easter is not that which follows upon suffering, freedom after the chains, satiety after hunger, reunion after separation. It is joy which lies beyond suffering and achievement. Suffering and joy are in perfect balance. Suffering is the opposite of joy; but joy is not the opposite of suffering.[8]

Healing Love

We have all discovered in past experiences how God became real as our Healer and Savior when in our sufferings and pain we cried out to a power beyond our strength. When reduced to a big zero in our broken-

Let go-let God ,

ness, we knew that hope in God alone could save us. No one has gone through life without experiencing some bodily brokenness. Before we die, we shall have known sleepless nights passed in writhing pain or fever. We shall have discovered also the presence of God's creative Word meeting us in our bodily ills. New life will have been poured into us as, backed up against an unsurmountable wall, we shall have surrendered ourselves to God's protective care.

No physical suffering can compare, however, to the mental agonies endured by us as we grappled against inner fears, anger, hatred, depression, or loneliness. Perhaps such anguish came in having been rejected in love or in the struggle entailed in letting go of our self-centered world to believe and trust and love the other.

Or perhaps the inner struggle will come in the deepest reaches of our spirit as demonic forces rise up in blackening clouds of despondency, blasphemous thoughts, doubts about God's existence and love for us.

In such trials, regardless of their causes or source, we are granted the occasion to rise from a "death" situation to enter into the conflict with such enemies to our true life. Diadochus of Photice of the sixth century summarizes the common belief of the Christian warriors of the desert when he wrote:

> In the same way as wax, unless heated and softened for long, cannot take the seal impressed upon it, even so man, unless tried with toils and weaknesses, cannot take in the seals of God's power. This is why the Lord says to St. Paul: "My grace is sufficient for you, for my power is made perfect in weakness" while the apostle himself boasts saying: "I will all the more gladly boast of my weaknesses that the power of Christ may rest upon me."[9]

In such sufferings the healing Word of God, Jesus Christ, again stretches out His hand of love to call us into a new sharing in His resurrectional life. He gently calls us out of our prison-tomb confinement to have our bonds loosed and to be set free of our death-dealing past.

Daily Miracles

Part of God's healing of us from our death-dealing past will come in the increase of faith, hope and love that His Word releases within us by the power of His Spirit. Such an increase will allow us to become converted like little children (Mk 10:13; Lk 9:46) and be gently receptive to

Baptism of Spirit

gift of knowledge

discover God in all things, especially in our sufferings and the non-being of our lives. Part of our sharing daily in the resurrection of Jesus will consist in our ability to see God everywhere. If He is in all the circumstances of our lives, He is acting out of love so that we can share in the power and glory He gave to His Son in His sufferings and death on our behalf.

The secret of our lives is to have the courage to suffer in hope in order to have the joy to live. Only if we are ready to let go of the obstacles in our lives that prevent our further growth in love, shall we be able to share in that greater possession of life.

Jesus never really gave His followers a well-worked out system of moral sayings or laws to be obeyed. He is the sole gift that He gives us by His death and resurrection. He lives within us through the Spirit that He released once He has completely died and risen from that death. And from within us and within the circumstances of our daily lives He operates with His love. He pours out His Spirit to give us courage and strength to bear all negative forces within us and outside of us. In His love we can do all things.

He continually invites us to rise from what would be merely negativity in our lives to a new oneness with His risen life. The Gospels are full of examples Jesus gave of what His resurrectional power could do to transform His followers into godly people.

> Love your enemies, do good to those who hate you, bless those who curse you, pray for those who treat you badly. To the man who slaps you on one cheek, present the other cheek too; to the man who takes your cloak from you, do not refuse your tunic. Give to everyone who asks you, and do not ask for your property back from the man who robs you. Treat others as you would like them to treat you. If you love those who love you, what thanks can you expect? . . . Instead, love your enemies and do good, and lend without any hope of return. You will have a great reward, and you will be sons of the Most High for he himself is kind to the ungrateful and the wicked. (Lk 6:27–35)

No one can effect the change from death-dealing to life-giving in your life except yourself in cooperation with the risen Lord and His Spirit of love. Today you will meet such opportunities in the strange mood that comes over you as you remember a friend from your past life, in the sharp word from a loved one that cuts you down, in the petty jealousy that seethes through your being as you look upon the successes of others.

God in His providential care allows "sufficient evil" of the day to come to all of us. But we must be able to see such occasions as God's "call" to us to come aside and share in a newness of being. He calls us to become in such circumstances His loving children.

Communal Resurrection

But our rising to a new life in Christ through transcendent love in our sufferings never effects a change solely in our own lives. As we rise to a new integration of our true self in Christ, we necessarily do so in the social context of our daily living toward others. We can become loving only in loving others. Thus our rising into a newness of resurrectional life with Christ, as we live more and more in Him and allow Him to live entirely in us, has an effect on those around us. Receiving within our hearts the love of God who has loved us to the madness of the cross, we become focal points of that same divine love to flow out toward all human beings whom we encounter.

> My dear People,
> since God has loved us so much,
> we too should love one another.
> No one has ever seen God;
> but as long as we love one another
> God will live in us
> and his love will be complete in us.
> We can know that we are living in him
> and he is living in us
> because he lets us share his Spirit....
> God is love
> and anyone who lives in love lives in God,
> and God lives in him.
> 1 Jn 4:11–16

Petru Dumitriu, the Rumanian novelist, has captured the divine presence in the miracle of each moment.

> A miracle is an everyday event which brings us into direct contact with the meaning of the world, and of God. If we are conscious of the divine nature of every happening and every fact, then everything

is miraculous. But it is hard not to forget. Consciousness flags in its perception of the divinity of the world, and we disregard the miraculous by taking it for granted. For those who worship God every event is a sign, and there are some signs which cannot be ignored.[10]

If God is so present and always acting out of love in the material world by His uncreated energies of love, can we, then, speak of a distinction between the sacred and the profane worlds? Can we even speak of something that is completely negative, disastrous, unsuccessful, a failure? Such concepts flow out of our insecure, false self that is not open to the presence of the resurrected Lord. But for the little children of this world, for those who by faith, hope, and love contemplate God at the heart of matter, "The world is charged with the grandeur of God. It will flame out, like shining from shook foil."[11]

Our human task is to search for the face of God in all things and to find our oneness with everything, in being all one in His trinitarian love. T.S. Eliot in his *Four Quartets* describes this human search for God as an ever new beginning:

> We shall not cease from exploration,
> And the end of all our exploring
> Will be to arrive where we started
> And know the place for the first time.[12]

As we learn to die to self and receive purity of heart so that we can see God everywhere, we can recognize by faith that God is present in all persons whom we meet, in all events happening in our material universe. He is present as transforming, deifying, loving energy moving to communion with us and through us to communion with the entire material world into a oneness in Christ Jesus. Jesus is becoming the risen Lord of the universe as we become signs of the new creation by the love we allow to shine forth from our lives into the lives of others.

As we experience the secret of life in death-resurrection in the ordinary events of daily living, we can go forth into a broken, dying world, "groaning in one great act of giving birth" (Rom 8:22), to bring forth the greatest miracle of all, the raising of the universe into the total Christ, His Body, fashioned from death to life, from suffering to purification, from isolation to communion in the Spirit of love.

A strange paradox occurs to such as have begun to live from suffering unto resurrectional life. Suffering becomes joy, death is new life. The presence of Christ is living within such Christians. And yet they are to be the midwife to bring forth Christ in other human beings. They look upon the suffering and broken ones of this world and in hope they see Christ. This oneness with Christ and the human scene does not gloss over the agonizing pain that our brothers and sisters are suffering. It becomes part of the miracle that, as we accept their sufferings and make them our own as Jesus did in His agony in the garden and on the cross, we become instruments for the miracle of resurrection to take place again, now in their lives.

The more defaced the image of God is in each man and woman, the more ardently does the true Christian wish to be used as a medium to recreate it, so that Jesus Christ shines forth with all His divine splendor latent in each human being. As God took a piece of this imperfect world and transfigured it into His glorious, risen Son, so now is the same power of the glorified Jesus, ever present in this struggling world, continuing to transform creation into a new Jerusalem. Yet the risen Lord needs us to bring about the continued miracle of death-resurrection, as we bring His raising power to those dead and dying.

A Leaven of Love

By His resurrection, Jesus Christ has irrevocably inserted Himself into our material world. He is like a powerful *enzyme*, drawing all men and women who freely accept His fermenting love. He stretches out through His Body, the Church, to touch and raise us into new life. He is present in the preached Word and in His sacraments. He is also present in His Spirit of love in every material event of our lives.

As we bring all of our death-dealing moments to His healing love and experience a new raising of ourselves into greater union with Him, we become also a leaven, permeated by God's very own enzymic love, living and transforming us from within. God asks us at every moment to enter into the brokenness of each person we are privileged to meet and serve lovingly in order to bring to them a share in the miracle of resurrection. There can be no greater humanizing force in our lives than to work consciously toward building up the risen Body of Christ in all power and glory. We and all other human beings around us are continuously in process, through our daily lives of activities and passivities, joys and sorrows, sin and reconciliation, of being raised up into becoming more and more God's loving children by becoming one in His only begotten Son. As we know ourselves in the Father's eternal love, we become the extension of His Son's Body, to bring others by our love and God's love in us into that Body.

We are guided daily by the vision of hope that Saint Paul gives us of the risen Lord who is reconciling all things to the Father. Even now as we learn to give up our brokenness to God's healing Word, and we experience a new sharing in Jesus' resurrection, we learn also to accept with love the brokenness in our neighbor. We hope in the ultimate victory of the risen Savior.

> Just as all men die in Adam, so all men will be brought to life in Christ; but all of them in their proper order: Christ as the first-fruits and then, after the coming of Christ, those who belong to him. After that will come the end, when he hands over the kingdom to God the Father, having done away with every sovereignty, authority and power. For he must be king until he has put all his enemies under his feet and the last of the enemies to be destroyed is death, for everything is to be put under his feet. Though when it is said that everything is subjected, this clearly cannot include the One who subjected everything to him. And when everything is subjected to him, then the Son himself will be subject in his turn to the One who subjected all things to him, so that God may be all in all. (1 Cor 15:22–28)

NOTES

1. For an historical treatment of this Easter icon, see Reinhold Lange, *The Resurrection*, trans. Hans Hermann Rosenwald, vol. 16 of *Pictorial Library of Eastern Church Art* (Recklinghausen: Aurel Bongers Publishers, 1967).

2. W.J. Turner, *Beethoven: The Search for Reality* (London: Ernest Benn, 1927).

3. Gabriel Marcel, *Being and Having* (London: Dacre Press, 1949), p. 124.

4. Ibid., p. 116.

5. Paul Tillich, *The Courage to Be* (New Haven: Yale University Press, 1952), p. 39.

6. Carl Jung, *The Integration of Personality* (London: Kegan Paul, 1940), p. 296.

7. H.A. Williams, *True Resurrection* (New York: Holt, Rinehart and Winston, 1972).

8. Simone Weil, *First and Last Notebooks* (Oxford: Oxford University Press, 1970), p. 69.

9. Diadochus of Photice, *One Hundred Chapters on Spiritual Perfection*, no. 94, trans. D.M. Freeman, in "Diadochus of Photice," *Diakonia* 7, no. 4 (1972): 348.

10. Petru Dumitriu, *Incognito*, trans. Norman Denny (London: Collins, 1964), p. 445.

11. G.M. Hopkins, "God's Grandeur," in *A Hopkins Reader*, ed. John Pick (New York/London: Oxford University Press, 1973), p. 13.

12. T.S. Eliot, *Four Quartets* (New York: Harcourt & Brace & Co., 1943), p. 39.

Chapter Four

DEATH IS RESURRECTION

Have you ever given much thought to the subject of *your* death, your passing definitively from this life into eternal life? Most of us ask the wrong questions when we ponder our deaths. We wonder when it will happen, at night or during daytime, in old age or at a relatively young age, in winter, summer, spring, or fall. Where will it take place, along a roadside, a victim of a car accident? Or perhaps in an airplane crash or in a bathtub? What details of the *how* will make up our death? Will it be a long, lingering dying from an incurable disease or a bad heart, or will it be sudden and unforeseen?

Saint Paul calls these "stupid" questions, especially the questions we might ask about what our bodies will look like in that life after death (1 Cor 15:36). The fact is certain: you and I shall surely one day die. That dying moment will be definitive, a "passing-over" into a new existence in a form different from that in which we now live. The details we cannot do much about, for they escape our control at this present moment and so often unfold through the interaction of many other persons and events. What is important is our Christian understanding of our final death so that we can have now the courage to live in the dialectic of death-resurrection, a present *now* experience of dying to our selfishness to rise even now to a new dynamic life in the risen Christ.

The Smell of Death

Everywhere we look around us we see not only birth but also signs of dying and death. Watching television and reading our newspapers, we see much of the violence, suddenness, and definitiveness of death. One reaction for many of us would be to block out the thought of death from our consciousness. Foolishly we might immerse ourselves in pleasures of this world, in our work, in sports, movies, travels, all in order to forget the apparent meaninglessness of death. We might yield to a fatalism that Jean-Paul Sartre expresses in *Nausea*: "I was thinking, that here we sit, all of us, eating and drinking to preserve our precious existence and really there is nothing, nothing, absolutely no reason for existing."[1]

We might strive, lacking any religious faith built upon God's revelation in Scripture and the teaching of the Christian Church, to defeat the awful sting of death and its apparent victory, through a humanitarianism that would seek to build a better world for future generations, even though this life on earth is the only one that will ever exist. A gross pessimism might incline us toward an escape into religion that might erroneously lead us away from God's presence in His material creation, into a false nirvana.

A Faulty Christian View

Even as Christians who pray Scripture and are in touch with the teachings of the Church as handed down in its tradition, we might entertain an erroneous view of death. Such a faulty view of death among Christians in times past and present often stems from a separation of the spiritual realms from those of the material. Through Platonism, Christians have wrongly accepted in their habitual view of death a definitive separation between the body and the soul in human death.

Have you not inherited from teachers and preachers an habitual understanding of human death as the definitive separation of the body from the soul? Death in such a view comes only to the material body that is mortal by its nature, while the soul by its nature is immortal and lives forever. The body dies, not the soul. The "person" is usually associated with the "soul," while the body, that in this life has not been conceived of as important but rather a "drag" warring against the soul, is confined to the grave where it remains until the day of resurrection. Resurrection in such a view is a static moment that occurs only at the end of the world; but such a view is no more than resuscitation, and not true Christian resurrection!

All too often in this view, presenting death only as a final moment at the end of our earthly life, we objectivize death and can handle it by placing it in the far distant future and therefore we seek never to think of it. The result is that we fail also to begin seriously to live.

A Christian Understanding of Death

As Christians, we must reject a literal interpretation of Platonism and even the imagery given in some of the biblical writings that would separate our bodies from our souls, as though two constitutive parts of us were physically wrenched from their unity into a separation that would last until resurrection day. By turning to a more biblical view of man, we can offset this gross literalness.

In Scripture, especially in the writings of Saint Paul, we see that the human person is made up of various relationships of a whole person to the world around him and to God. Saint Paul calls man *soma* in his understanding of a whole person as a psychophysical unity, a personality turned toward the created world around him. The *pneuma*, or spirit, is the total man viewed in his unique personality through a knowing relationship in love to God. Man relates to the cosmic world, not only through the body (*soma*) which is made up of the soul or *psyche* with all the emotions and passions we call irascible and concupiscible, but also through the *sarx* or flesh. He relates also to the material world through the *pneuma* or spirit, which is, however, more transcendent in its relationship to God in a conscious self-giving act of love toward God.[2]

In such a biblical view, death is a rather sudden disruption of man's relationship to the material world through the *sarx* or flesh. The *sarx* condition is more than our mere materiality or flesh; it contains an element of propensity toward self-centeredness. The *sarx* condition that comes through the limitations of being in the "flesh" is lost in death, even though the habits of selfishness acquired in that earthly existence remain.

Death is one of the most dramatic events in our evolution as human beings. It allows us definitively to move into a greater consciousness through a dying to the vegetable and animal life in us. Such a whole person, the biblical *soma*, the body-man, in his personality toward the world, now becomes more open to the whole universe.

Karl Rahner, in a very creative essay entitled "On the Theology of Death," seeks to show that not the body but the whole person dies. He seeks to avoid the understanding that the soul leaves this world and takes flight into a spiritual realm, losing all relationships with the material world.

> It should rather be borne in mind that, even in her lifetime, as informing the body, the spiritual soul is an open system toward the world. It might also be remembered with profit that natural philoso-

phy finds it almost impossible to restrict the idea of the human "body" to what is covered by the skin. The spiritual soul, moreover, through her essential relationship to the body, is basically open to the world in such a manner that she is never a monad without windows, but always in communication with the whole of the world. [3]

Such modern authors, as Karl Rahner, Paul Chauchard and others, [4] seek to show that the human person in death moves higher to where he or she relates in greater intensity both *outward* toward the cosmic world through an expanding awareness of his or her solidarity with the material world, and in greater intensity inward toward God in a greater realization of his or her unique being in relationship to Him.

An authentic Christian view of death should stress that the whole human person undergoes death. Jesus, not merely His body, died. We shall totally undergo, as a complete entity, as a person, the experience of death. But death is a "passing-over" to a new level of human growth. What is most important in a proper view of our physical death is that we shall continue to be the same persons we were while on this earth, enjoying the same level of consciousness, bringing into the life to come the same good and bad habits, knowing and communicating with other human beings through the relationships developed in this earthly life through our body, soul, and spirit relationships.

Why Death?

Why do we have to die? Will science ever perfect the process of preventing deteriorization of human living cells so that we may reach a state of never dying? From Holy Scripture and the teaching of the Church we are taught that death is a result of sin. Man, before he had sinned and was driven out of the garden of Eden (Gen 3:23), could have lived immune from death or, if he *were* to die, such a transition into a higher level of conscious evolution would have been likened move to a sleep than to the violent upheaval which because of sin it now is.

What has sin added to death? To answer this we must distinguish between the active and the passive elements in our death. Death is something all human beings must undergo passively. It happens to us, whether we like it or not. Even this experience could have happened to the first man and woman had they not sinned. It is the biological aspect that brings to a definitive end our "natural" way of existing through a material body in space-and-time-relationships to the rest of the material world around us.

But our death also holds out the possibility of an "active" element. This is where our human decision enters into our death process. It concerns our attitude of how we accept our "fate" of dying and move to a new level of self-surrendering love toward God and other persons. We can see how this element is very much determined by our earthly acts of accepting the "death-dealing" situations and transforming them into "life-giving," loving opportunities.

Karl Rahner well highlights this active acceptance of death:

> But how he dies his death and how he understands it, depends on the decision of his freedom. Here he does not carry something imposed on him, but what he chooses himself. That is to say: in the deed of the dying existence, man is necessarily free in his attitude toward death. Although he has to die, he is asked how he wishes to do it. For, existence conscious of itself must unavoidably see the end. It sees this end all through life, perhaps dimly and not explicitly. It may happen that it will purposely avoid looking at it, or it will simply overlook it (but still will realize it all the same). Inasmuch as man freely takes upon himself this existence tending toward the end, he also freely accepts the movement toward the end.[5]

Death for us, who live under the sign of the wages of sin, contains fearful elements. We find it most difficult to believe and trust in the power of God to lead us over from death to a new life. No matter how much we have prayed in life for deeper faith, hope, and love in God and His caring for us, so that all things, even death, can work unto good if we love Him (Rom 8:28), there will always remain areas of dark foreboding and fear of what awaits us in the process of final death.

You can admit with Saint Paul that Christ has conquered sin and death and therefore you should not feel any longer any sting from death which has lost its victory over you (1 Cor 15:55). Still in that ultimate moment of "passing-over," you can never be sure of how you will react. The "wages of sin" (Rom 6:23) lie deeply within us, in the fiber of our being, and in every past decision made during our earthly life. That final moment flows out of the collection of all the previous *now moments* in which we actively and freely choose to determine to live out of self-sacrificing love toward God and neighbor.

Sweet Death

Just as we have seen that sufferings and trials are most helpful in calling out of us new powers that become actuated in transcendent love, so the greatest suffering, our physical death, can become for us the greatest concentration of self-surrendering in loving trust and abandonment to God. But the decision to live for God as a gift, in return to Him who has infinitely loved us in His manifested love for us shown by His dying Son, Jesus Christ, can be made only in the light of the daily decisions we must make in order to respond to the love of God as it is revealed to us in the context of our ordinary living.

This is what Jesus and the early disciples of the New Testament preached. The *now* moment is the only locus or place where, as we choose to live in self-sacrificing love for others, we can accept death freely and replace it with a sharing in the resurrection of Jesus. Not to obey this "command" of Jesus is to reject God's spoken Word to us.

And yet our modern age has developed a false optimism about what to expect in death and dying. The dying experience is painted in terms of the psychological euphoria that certain "dying" patients underwent in a close-to-death experience, which never really became definitive death for them, and they "return" to tell us of the joy they felt in "passing over" to the other side. Dr. Elizabeth Kubler-Ross, Dr. R.A. Moody, Dr. Karlis Osis and his assistant, Dr. Erlendur Haraldsson, and many others[6] have done much to create an optimism regarding what we should expect in our final death. There is one danger: such naive optimism might lessen the pangs of sin and the reality of death, not only as a punishment, but also as the most important moment of full, personal decision at the time when a human being strives in the throes of death to reach total self-realization. But its greatest danger is to put off a dynamic response to death-resurrection in the given moment that we naively think separates our death from the context of all our earlier, earthly experiences and free choices.

The Death of Jesus

Jesus, not only taught us to be attentive and repent of our false ways of viewing reality, especially in our own holding on to our untrue self, but He lived out this alertness to death-new life, as circumstances brought Him into conflict and "temptations" to live or to die to His own self-interests and to live in loving surrender to His Heavenly Father. The magnificent obsession in His earthly life was centered around doing only His

Father's will. As He progressively experienced the Father's love, working itself out in self-giving to Him in the events of each day (Jn 5:17), He learned to surrender Himself to that loving presence of His Father. It was in His "heart," in the deepest reaches of His consciousness, in the depths of His being, in the core at His center, that He contemplated His Father who loved Him and begot Him in His humanity according to His own image. As Jesus let go of His life in loving submission to the Father loving Him in total self-giving, He grew in the consciousness of which He spoke in His prayer to the Father (Jn 17:21–23).

As Jesus prayerfully allowed the Father's love to enter into all levels of His consciousness and unconsciousness, much as the story of His temptations in the desert shows, He learned to let go of the control He exercised over His own human existence. He experienced at one and the same time the immense love of the Father and the ontological necessity of returning that love in an abandonment that would lead eventually to His ignominious death on the cross. Especially in the agony of Gethsemane and on the cross, Jesus entered into the black darkness of His inner self and there struggled with the test of His identity. Was He to worship the Lord God and serve Him alone (Dt 6:13; Mt 4:10) or was He to yield to fear and doubt and in self-centeredness grasp to hold on to His life?

His whole life at each moment was a preparation for His final death. Each choice was made in ever-growing freedom to place His life, every thought, word, and deed, under the good pleasure of His Father. He was like us, tempted in all things save sin (Heb 4:15), for no one could convict Him of sin (Jn 8:26). There was no injustice in Him (Jn 7:18) because He always did what pleased His Heavenly Father (Jn 8:29).

Jesus submitted every thought, word, and deed to the good pleasure of His Father and entered into an inner dying process to win progressively the gift of freedom through a new victory of loving, self-abandonment to His Father. Freedom for Jesus, as for us, is God's gift through the Spirit of love, but it is won by a great struggle wherein the isolated self surrenders to the true self in love, freely given. Without conflict, even in the development of Jesus' human freedom, there could have been no growth in freedom, in love and in His full personhood.

Love is an Emptying

It is in Jesus' final death on the cross that we begin to understand something of the dialectic of death-resurrection. As we prayerfully encounter Jesus, not only in His historical act of suffering and dying on the hill outside Jerusalem, but also in His ever present *kairos* moment of *now* in which He is continually made present to us in faith dying freely out of love for us, we open up to the possibility of sharing in His death-resurrection.

Jesus was not a victim caught in an inescapable fate, a net woven by the political intrigues of the contemporaries who put Him to death. He was becoming free as He took His life and offered it freely to be disposed of according to the wish and good pleasure of His Father. He actively surrendered His life out of love on our behalf to image as healing love His eternal Father's infinite love for all of us. "The Father loves me because I lay down my life in order to take it up again. No one takes it from me; I lay it down of my own free will" (Jn 10:17).

On the cross, His hour was approaching when the Son of Man would be lifted up and would draw all mankind to Himself (Jn 3:13). He was passing over from His human potential for fully expressed love as He freely surrendered His life to the Father on our behalf. Actively He gathered up every loving moment of His earlier life that He lived to please His Father and not burst beyond the bonds of any self-centeredness into a new-found love that can only be expressed in the phrase *death-resurrection*. The Spirit of the Father's love anointed Him and empowered Him to manifest toward the Father on our behalf a human love that would be the most perfect expression in human form of the Father's love for Him.

A Suffering Servant

It is in the death-hymn of the messianic Psalm 22 that the Spirit of God brings us to a new depth of Jesus' love for us. In contemplating the Suffering Servant of Yahweh, foretold in the prophecies of Deutero-Isaiah (Is 42:52–53), we can receive the Spirit's revelation about the infinite depths of the Father's love for each of us.[7]

The first part is the cry of Jesus to His Father in the darkness of abandonment that came over His human consciousness. The sky darkened and the raucous soldiers stopped in their ribaldry and mocking jests. Earth, sky, and air suddenly froze in a mute stare at the white figure hanging on the cross. A cry pierced the darkened silence:

My God, my God, why have you deserted me?
How far from saving me, the words I groan!
I call all day, my God, but you never answer,
all night long I call and cannot rest.

Ps 22:1–2

"Eli . . . Eli . . ." At this moment the Father of Jesus who had always been a light, bathing Him with His smiling love, now seems clouded in fierce darkness. How Jesus must have thrilled at His baptism and at the transfiguration to have heard those words of loving approval from His Father, "This is my Son, the Beloved; my favour rests on him" (Mt 3:17). But now it is as though the Father's wrath is poured out against Him. Jesus feels the quagmire of the world's sinful filth suck Him down and cover Him with darkness.

As Jesus surrenders completely to His Father's will, soft rays of light move toward the darkness just as the first sign of dawn with its velvet touch dissolves the darkness of night. In Jesus' despairing abandonment, groping to look again upon the countenance of the Father whom He adored so profoundly, He experiences the paradox He had preached to others: "Happy those who mourn: they shall be comforted" (Mt 5:5).

Do not stand aside, Yahweh.
O my strength, come quickly to my help; . . .
Then I shall proclaim your name to my brothers,
praise you in full assembly:
you who fear Yahweh, praise him!
Entire race of Jacob, glorify him!
Entire race of Israel, revere him!
For he has not despised
or disdained the poor man in his poverty,
has not hidden his face from him
but has answered him when he called.

Ps 22:19, 22–4

The Pass-over

On the cross Jesus receives the full release of the Father's Spirit of love that poured over His whole being, bathing Him in a new-found oneness with the Father. Jesus, dying on the cross for love of us human beings, *passes over* into His new, resurrectional existence, not after three days but immediately as He dies to the last holding on to His existence. Death is Resurrection! When love reaches its peak, it moves immediately from death to aloneness in order to enter into a new union with the one loved.

Jesus said: ". . . for as the lightning flashing from one part of heaven lights up the other, so will be the Son of Man when his day comes. But first he must suffer grievously and be rejected by this generation" (Lk 17:24–25). His sufferings and death were intimately linked with His exaltation (Mk 10:36–40). We see that He often links His death and resurrection with the fulfillment of the Kingdom of God (Mk 8:31–32; 9:9–12; 10:10:10:32–34). It is certainly Saint Luke's understanding of the sufferings and death and resurrection of Christ when he presents the risen Lord as instructing the disciples on the road to Emmaus: "You foolish men! So slow to believe the full message of the prophets! Was it not ordained that the Christ should suffer and so enter into his glory?" (Lk 24:25–26).

The *kerygma* or preaching of the early Church, as found in the Gospels and Pauline writings, clearly attests to the necessity for Jesus to serve unto humiliating death so that He might enter into glory. On Pentecost Saint Peter preached: "For this reason the whole House of Israel can be certain that God has made this Jesus whom you crucified both Lord and Christ" (Acts 2:36). Peter, like so many of us, wanted a glorious, risen Jesus but without suffering because he (just like us) did not enjoy the thought of himself sharing in the ignominy of a crucified Leader. Jesus taught that such service unto death was a part of God's plan whereby we would be healed of our selfishness as the Spirit revealed to us the fiery love of the triune God for each of us. "For me He died," we can cry out with Saint Paul (Gal 2:20).

The first Christian communities professsed that Jesus was one with God, His equal from all eternity, but, out of loving service for us, He surrendered that power and glory. He did this precisely so that He could be like us in all things. "God dealt with sin by sending his own Son in a body as physical as any sinful body, and in that body God condemned sin" (Rom 8:3–4). And for this reason the Father was well pleased in the death of Jesus: now for all time the love of the invisible God has been made manifest unto the last drop of blood in the suffering servant, Jesus. Here is the Image of God's love for us! Who sees Jesus dying for us, sees the Father's great love for us (Jn 14:9).

And so Saint Paul sends to the Church of the Philippians a hymn of praise that well expresses the antinomy of the death-resurrection of Jesus:

> His state was divine
> yet he did not cling
> to his equality with God
> but emptied himself
> to assume the condition of a slave,
> and become as men are;
> and being as all men are
> he was humbler yet, even to accepting death,
> death on a cross.
> But God raised him high
> and gave him the name
> which is above all other names
> so that all beings
> in the heavens, in earth and in the underworld,
> should bend the knee at the name of Jesus
> and that every tongue should acclaim
> Jesus Christ as Lord,
> to the glory of God the Father.
>
> Phil 2:6–11

God reaches the peak of speaking His Word. He can be no more present as Love to us human beings than in His Image, Jesus Christ, the outcast, rejected, made sin and poured out on the cross, even to the last drop of blood.

Light Found in Darkness

Jesus met His greatest temptation to find His meaning in Himself or in loving service for us to please the Father. In the face of the imminent death that slowly choked life from every cell in His Body, Jesus must have wondered about the significance of His life, the years of monotonous living at Nazareth, the preaching unto fatigue only to be clawed by the broken ones of the earth who wanted His healing touch and then, His agony and crucifixion. For us, also, death will be the greatest threat to existence.

He learned obedience to His Father and love was created in His heart for all of us as He hoped that His sufferings and death would bring life to every man, woman, and child created by His Father according to Him, the Father's own image (Col 1:15). Jesus freely gave Himself in life and in death to serve others. When on the cross hope seemed all but extinguished that His sacrifice would be meaningful to the human race, the Father "raised him high" (Phil 2:9). So the resurrection of Jesus must not be diluted of its power and true glory by relegating it to a return of His soul to His body. Nor is the resurrection simply the historical person, Jesus, continuing as if He had not died.

The whole Jesus died, not merely His body. The whole Jesus gave Himself for love of each of us. And the Father raised Him to new life and in that new life we also can now share.

> Blessed be God the Father of our Lord Jesus Christ, who in his great mercy has given us a new birth as his sons, by raising Jesus Christ from the dead, so that we have a sure hope and the promise of an inheritance that can never be spoilt or soiled and never fade away, because it is being kept for you in the heavens. (1 Pt 1:3–4)

During all His earthly life Jesus had been the Light, shining in the darkness of sinful brokenness. But now the fullness of His light shone brightly for all to see and to experience. On the pages of the New Testament joy is expressed everywhere because the early Christians believed that Jesus had gone forward into a completely new existence which He now makes possible for His followers to share.

Immortality Shared Even Now

The risen Jesus even now shares with us His glory and power that subject sin and death and all other powers of darkness to His dominion. We should refuse to be concerned with the wrong questions of when, where, how we will die and what our resurrected bodies will look like. Rather we should continually seek to answer by our new lives in the risen Lord: How can I live this moment in the death-resurrection of Jesus? How can I be led from fear and anxiety into being a true child of God, freed from my selfishness, and death, and the false values of the world around me so as to live in the freedom of the risen people of God?

Jesus, Victor over death, conquers our hearts, inspiring us to surrender to Him as Lord of our lives. He becomes the inner force that guides us in all our thoughts, words, and actions. Freedom is the progressive surrender in love to Him so that in each moment He is Lord.

We can even now share in His immortal life that brings us an inner, life-giving knowledge of the Father and Jesus, His son, through the Holy Spirit (Jn 17:3). We shall certainly die a physical death. But we believe that even now death has no hold or victory over us since we are totally a new creation in Christ (2 Cor 5:17). We believe that the death of Jesus is the death of God and the Father's infinite love for us is witnessed to by Jesus' passing-over from death into resurrection. His Spirit is poured out abundantly into our hearts as love (Rom 5:5) and in that Spirit we know we will live forever the life that is the life of the risen Christ, already living within us.

> Though your body may be dead it is because of sin, but if Christ is in you then your spirit is life itself because you have been justified; and if the Spirit of him who raised Jesus from the dead is living in you, then he who raised Jesus from the dead will give life to your own mortal bodies through his Spirit living in you. (Rom 8:10–11)

Immortality, as we find the concept preached in the New Testament, does not mean the absence of physical death. Rather it refers to our human sharing in the divine life of God Himself, a sharing which began in our lives at the very moment of our Baptism and continues each moment of our conscious life as we strive to yield to the guidance of the Spirit of the risen Jesus. This life is *already* ours to the degree that we die to self-love and rise to a new oneness in Christ shown each time we live in unselfish love for others.

Father Pierre Benoit summarized Saint Paul's evolutive thought on resurrection as an already event that can grow infinitely as we live in Christ:

> But he [Paul] gives the impression that while he abided by the traditional affirmation of the last resurrection, he regards it as less and less important and believes that the essential has already come to pass. His eschatology, which at the outset was "futurist," has become increasingly one that has already been effected.[8]

Living the Paschal Victory

Christians, who have begun to experience in their lives the dialectic of death-resurrection that Jesus, risen and living within them makes possible, go forth to witness to a materialistic world that God, through Jesus Christ, has entered into death and has conquered it in Christ's humanity. Such Christians have put on Christ. They live in and with Christ. Hence Christ's power in them is overcoming any corruption and sin and death to God's immortal life living within them.

With the Prophet Hosea, they can shout out the words of the promised Messiah: "And am I to save them from the power of Sheol? Am I to rescue them from Death? Where is your plague, Death? Where are your scourges, Sheol?" (Hos 13:13–14). The risen Jesus truly is entering daily into the Sheol of our lives and there is raising us up into new, immortal, and divine life. This is the summary of Saint Paul's understanding of the power of the risen Lord to effect even now immortality in our lives.

> When this perishable nature has put on imperishability, and when this mortal nature has put on immortality, then the words of scripture will come true. Death is swallowed up in victory. Death, where is your victory? Death, where is your sting? Now the sting of death is sin, and sin gets its power from the Law. So let us thank God for giving us the victory through our Lord Jesus Christ. Never give in then, my dear brothers, never admit defeat; keep on working at the Lord's work always, knowing, that in the Lord, you cannot be labouring in vain. (1 Cor 15:54–58)

We are to reckon ourselves to be already dead, dead unto sin, but alive unto God through Jesus Christ our Lord (Rom 6:11). We are moving moment by moment into greater integration and fulfillment of the powers God planted in our nature when He created us and bestowed upon us in Baptism the seed of His very own divine life. We are freed from the fear of final death. Our resurrection is already a reality as we witness by every word and gesture that Jesus Christ is risen and dies no more (Rom 6:9–10). "Let your thoughts be on heavenly things, not on the things that are on earth, because you have died, and now the life you have is hidden with Christ in God." (Col 3:2–3).

We share now in His risen life. In hope and joy and love, we are to share this reality with all who are heavily burdened with suffering, above all, with those in sin and in the throes of final death. And we have absolute proof that we have passed from death unto life: ". . . we have passed out of death and into life, and of this we can be sure because we love our brothers" (1 Jn 3:14). We strive at each moment and in each event of our daily lives to live in the commandments of Jesus Christ. "I tell you most solemnly, whoever keeps my word will never see death" (Jn 8:51). Obedience to Jesus Christ is the answer we give to the world of suffering and dying. And this means, not that death brings us ultimately to our resurrection, but that *death is resurrection*, right now. And in Jesus Christ, risen, is the great IS that makes our dying to selfishness and isolation the very same experience as sharing in His resurrection that is God's life in us. We share this with others as we love them into a sharing also of the same resurrectional life by the love that we have for them: ". . . as long as we love one another God will live in us and his love will be complete in us" (1 Jn 4:12).

NOTES

1. Jean-Paul Sartre, *Nausea* (N.Y.: New Directions, 1964), p. 112.

2. I have developed these concepts in *The Everlasting Now* (South Bend, Ind.: Ave Maria Press, 1980), pp. 18–19, 180–81. Much in this present chapter can be found in the ideas expressed in that book.

3. Karl Rahner, *On the Theology of Death*, trans. Charles H. Henkey (N.Y.: Herder and Herder, 1961), p. 30.

4. See Paul Chauchard, *Man and Cosmos*, trans. George Courtright (New York: Herder and Herder, 1965), p. 143; Jose-Maria Gonzales-Ruiz, "Should We De-Mythologize the Separated Soul," in *The Problem of Eschatology*, vol. 41 of *Concilium* (New York: Paulist Press, 1969), pp. 82–96; also, Anton Grabner-Haider, "The Biblical Understanding of 'Resurrection' and 'Glorification,'" ibid., pp. 66–81.

5. Karl Rahner, op. cit., pp. 93–94.

6. See E. Kübler-Ross, *On Death and Dying* (New York: Macmillan Co., 1969); idem, *Questions and Answers on Death and Dying* (New York: Macmillan Co., 1974); idem, *Death: The Final Stage of Growth* (Englewood Cliffs, N.J.: Prentice-Hall, 1975); R.A. Moody, *Life After Death* (Atlanta: Mockingbird Books, 1975); idem, *Reflections on Life After Death* (Atlanta: Mockingbird Books, 1977); Dr. Karlis Osis and Dr. Erlendur Haraldsson, *What They Saw . . . At the Hour of Death* (New York: Avon Books, 1977).

7. Jürgen Moltmann confirms this understanding of Jesus' fulfillment of Ps. 22; see *The Crucified God* (N.Y.: Harper and Row, 1974), pp. 146–47.

8. Pierre Benoit, O.P., "Resurrection: At the End of Time or Immediately after Death?" in *Immortality and Resurrection*, vol. 60 of *Concilium* (New York: Herder and Herder, 1970), pp. 103–14.

Chapter Five

THE RISEN LORD
AND THE EUCHARIST

Have you ever noticed what a difference takes place in your relationships with friends when they invite you to eat a meal at their
table? They buy food and carefully prepare it. Possibly they serve you a
good table wine to warm your heart. As they offer you food and drink,
they are saying symbolically: "By this food and drink we offer you our
love. We want to nourish new life in you by sharing ourselves with you,
our love, our presence in your life."

   In no physical sense are they or their love for you the food and drink
nor are they in any way literally inside the nourishment they offer you.
And yet in their loving self-giving they become present to you in the
"breaking of the bread." The food and drink are symbol-carriers making
it possible to "act out" in a physical, visible action a *ritual*, a hidden,
mysterious spiritual reality that we call love. Human interiority is not
only expressed through such actions but the inside feelings and move-
ments become a transforming power far beyond what was locked up inside the human heart.

The Gift of God
   The Eucharist is the *locus* or place in our human space and time where,
in a similar "meal," God reaches, as it were, the peak of His inner
trinitarian love of the Father, Son, and Holy Spirit. The tremendous
mutual self-giving of Father and Son in their Spirit of love cannot con-
tain itself. It wants to burst forth, to be shared with others. God gives
Himself to us created beings in His many gifts.

Yet all such symbols of His self-giving to us are inadequate expressions of the total gift in love. As the Trinity seeks to share its very own intimate "family" life with us, the Word leaps forth from out of the heart of the Father. "For when peaceful stillness compassed everything and the night in its swift course was half spent, your all-powerful word from heaven's royal throne bounded, a fierce warrior into the doomed land" (Wis 18:14–15).

God's Word inserts Himself into our material world, taking upon Himself the form of a servant (Phil 2:8), like to us in all things save sin (Heb 4:15). Not only does God wed Himself to the entire, material universe by assuming matter into the trinitarian family, but God also touches each of us human beings. Objectively through the Incarnation, by His becoming the *New Adam*, the true Father of the renewed human race, Jesus Christ makes us all one.

In the Eucharist we are privileged to actualize this interiority of the Divine Trinity by eating of the Body of Jesus Christ and drinking His Blood. We come to the banquet table of the Lord and partake of the meal that is life-giving food. In giving us in the Eucharist His very body and blood as food and drink, Jesus Christ wishes to share His very own life with us.

> As I, who am sent by the living Father,
> myself draw life from the Father,
> so whoever eats me will draw life from me.
> This is the bread come down from heaven;
> not like the bread our ancestors ate:
> they are dead,
> but anyone who eats this bread
> will live for ever.
>
> Jn 6:57–58

The Father has the fullness of life and He has communicated it to His Son. Jesus Christ, the Image of the Father in human form, pours His very own life into all of us who wish to partake of His flesh and blood. He is the "Living Bread," the Bread of Life that comes down from Heaven. In the Incarnation He took upon Himself our human flesh; in the Eucharist we become assimilated into His human-divine being.

It is staggering to our weak human minds and impossible to comprehend adequately the depths of the Father's love for us as imaged in His only begotten Son. It is *in fact* that we become one with God's only Son. The gift of Himself that He gives us as our nourishing food in a new order of things transforms us into Himself. We are *engrafted* into His very being as a branch is inserted into the mainstream of the vine and become one total being (Jn 15:1–6). The early Fathers were lyrical in their expression of infinite love the Trinity pours out toward us in the Eucharist, as Saint John Chrysostom illustrates:

> Therefore in order that we may become of His Body, not in desire only, but also in very fact, let us become commingled with the Body. This, in truth, takes place by means of the food which He has given us as a gift, because He desired to prove the love which He has for us. It is for this reason that He has shared Himself with us and has brought His Body down to our level, namely, that we might be one with Him as the body is joined with the head.
>
> And to show the love He has for us He has made it possible for those who desire, not merely to look upon Him, but even to touch Him and to consume Him and to fix their teeth in His Flesh and to be commingled with Him; in short, to fulfill all their love. Let us, then, come back from that table like lions breathing out fire, thus becoming terrifying to the Devil and remaining mindful of our Head and of the love which He has shown us.[1]

A Meal to be Eaten

In the last supper that Jesus ate with His disciples before His death, He took bread and blessed it, broke it and gave it to them, as He said: "This is my body which will be given for you, do this as a memorial of me." He did the same with the cup of wine: "This cup is the new covenant in my blood which will be poured out for you" (Lk 22:19–20).

Saint Luke describes the first Christian community that gathered in Jerusalem as a group that "remained faithful to the teaching of the Apostles, to the brotherhood, to *the breaking of the bread* and to the prayers" (Acts 2:42). "The breaking of the bread" is the term which that Christian community used for the Eucharist.

That eucharistic meal did recall the last supper of Jesus and His complete self-giving to us unto the death of the cross. But that same meal also recalled Jesus' resurrection from the dead and the meals that He participated in with His disciples after His resurrection. The Eucharist, as a present-day ritual, retains this double aspect of Jesus' death and resurrection which the early Christians saw and experienced in the Eucharist as complements to each other.

Death-Resurrection

Jesus in the last supper ritually surrendered Himself to each member of the human race by giving Himself, as mysteriously present, in the gifts of bread and wine. He actualized that loving surrender by dying the next day on the cross.

Yet the disciples in the resurrectional apparitions ate meals with Jesus. Jesus "broke bread" and gave Himself to them, not in His dying, but in His risen body and life-giving blood. The Eucharist today brings us Jesus as immolated victim who dies for love of us. He is the sacrifice to the last drop of blood that takes away our sins.

Still the immolated Christ has passed over in His dying moment unto a new and glorious existence. We receive Christ as dying for us but also as already risen in glory. In the Eucharist Jesus is able to communicate Himself to us as *death-resurrection*. He now exists in the Eucharist, not as one who merely died for love of us, but as one who, in dying, has been raised up by the Father through the power of the Spirit and who now can communicate to us a share in His death-resurrection.

A Living Sacrifice

It is the Holy Spirit who makes the Eucharist possible. The Spirit establishes Jesus in the ever-now moment of dying and rising. It is through the Spirit that we are empowered to enter into the new way in which Jesus continues to give Himself to us in His death-glorification.

Just as the Holy Spirit was present in the Incarnation, effecting a begetting by the Father of His Son in human form (Lk 1:35), so the Holy Spirit is present in two ways in the Eucharist. The first way, highlighted in most of the Eastern Liturgies, is called the *epiklēsis*. This literally means a "calling down" of the Holy Spirit to bless and transform the gifts of bread and wine into the body and blood of Jesus Christ. "Send down your Holy Spirit upon us and upon these gifts lying before us . . . and make this bread the precious Blood of your Christ, Amen. Having changed them by your Holy Spirit, Amen, Amen, Amen."[2]

The second presence of the Holy Spirit is the bond of unity between the Father and the Son and all who receive Jesus Christ. This is called the *Koinōnia* or fellowship or communion of the Holy Spirit. This fruit of the Eucharist, prayed for in the Eastern Liturgies, is mentioned by Saint Paul: "The grace of the Lord Jesus Christ, the love of God and the fellowship of the Holy Spirit be with you all" (2 Cor 13:13).

Our sharing in the "fellowship" of the Holy Spirit allows us to enter into the eternal love action of Jesus as He is ever offering Himself to us in total sacrifice and in an uplifting of us to share in His now-moment resurrection to the degree that we also die to sin and live in the Spirit's gift of Jesus risen.

A High Priest Forever

The Epistle to the Hebrews presents the risen Christ as caught up in Heaven where He is permanently offering Himself to the Father as Priest and Victim on our behalf (Heb 8:1–4).

> He, on the other hand, has offered one single sacrifice for sins, and then taken his place for ever, at the right hand of God, where he is now waiting until his enemies are made into a footstool for him. By virtue of that one single offering, he has achieved the eternal perfection of all whom he is sanctifying. (Heb 10:12–14)

The Father accepts the sacrifice that Christ, the High Priest, is eternally offering of Himself on our behalf, and for this reason the Father raises Him in glory (Phil 2:10). The resurrection and glorification of Jesus occur at the very moment when the Father accepts Jesus' dying gift of Himself for our sakes.[3] F. X. Durrwell summarizes this teaching from the Epistle to the Hebrews:

> Though the sacrificial act took place in the past, its conclusion is something ever actual in the everlasting glorifying welcome of God. The act of passing from this world to the Father took place once for all, but the meeting with the Father continues forever; the victim is fixed eternally at the high point of the offering.... The final phase begins and remains at the exact moment of the sacrifice's being consummated. Christ stays at the high point of his priestly function, the offering of his death becomes eternal in the divinizing acceptance which crowns it.[4]

Saint John's Gospel has many passages that link up Christ's death and resurrection, His sacrifice that is not death but life-giving. "When you have lifted up the Son of Man, then you will know that I am He and that I do nothing of myself" (Jn 8:28). Jesus risen appears to the apostle, Thomas, and shows His wounds that He retains in His glorious, risen body. Jesus in glory is always in a high-priestly act of offering Himself as Victim unto the death of the cross. As the Father eternally accepts His death, Jesus is continually being exalted by that acceptance through which the Father glorifies the total Christ as His beloved Son.

The author of the Book of Revelation also associates the Lamb in Heaven with Christ the Victim and Christ in glory: "Then I saw . . . a Lamb that seemed to have been sacrificed. . . . worthy to be given power, riches, wisdom, strength, honor, glory and blessing" (Rev 5:6, 12).

Jesus Christ, both in Heaven and in the Eucharist, receives universal power and dominion over the entire universe precisely as He continually immolates Himself on our behalf. His reign begins in the death-resurrection moment caught in Heaven forever and is symbolized and effected in the Eucharist as we accept to live in His love-sacrifice unto glory.

In the Eucharist we, the members of Christ's body, join Him in the sacrifice. With Him we also perform the role of priest and victim, making a total offering of ourselves within the total community of the Church together with Christ, our High Priest. We offer Christ, the Victim, and ourselves, not only through the hands of the priest, but also with the priest by virtue of our own "royal priesthood" (1 Pet 2:9) received in Baptism.

The Fulfillment of all the Sacraments

In all the sacraments we can experience various *places* in our lives where we can encounter the dying-rising Jesus Christ. When we cooperate and the visible rite is properly celebrated, Jesus comes to us and brings us a new share in divine life. But specifically each sacrament brings us the divine life as applied in a very special way so that we can more perfectly live our redeemed life in Christ. In the Eucharist we receive Jesus as He prolongs His death and resurrection in us. We receive His life that enables us to share in our daily life in His death and resurrection.

The Eucharist, therefore, is the peak of all other sacramental encounters with Christ. It brings us into perfect union with the dying-rising Christ of glory who makes us partakers through the full release of His Spirit in His mysteries, in His life, in His Mystical Body. He grants us fervor in the service of God, fidelity in the observance of His laws, ever increasing sanctification. This completes a continuous redemption until the full development of the seed of immortality, the life of God in us, has reached its maturity.

The Eucharist completes all other sacraments insofar as it is already a sharing in the *parousia*, the final manifestation of the Lord in glory. Although we are still pilgrims moving through the desert of life, while at the same time we stretch out in hope for that everlasting city that awaits us, nevertheless, we already share somewhat in the final goal. The Eucharist is the full coming of the Lord in glory, the same as His final coming. And yet we proclaim in the Eucharist death, and resurrection, and His perfect glory until He comes. "Until the Lord comes, therefore, every time you eat this bread and drink this cup, you are proclaiming his death" (1 Cor 11:26).

We possess in the Eucharist the final goal of redemption and yet we possess it in truth and in anticipation, "already" and "not yet" in its fullness. The coming of Jesus in the Eucharist is a real coming in glory, having all the attributes of His final coming, and yet the Church-community, receiving the Bread of Life, longs ardently, even in the very moment of receiving the risen Savior, to see and possess Him in a still fuller manner.

To receive the Eucharist is to celebrate the *Pascha*, as the early Church fondly called the Eucharist and the feast of the resurrection. *Pascha* is the Aramaic derivation of the Hebrew word, *Pesach*, which means "passover." The Eucharist, as the celebration of the Passover, highlights, not only the goal or the final *Parousia*, but it shoots roots down through the ages to embrace all of God's chosen People, beginning with the Israelites who, in their enslavement to the Egyptians, were delivered by God as they "passed over" in the exodus into the desert and finally into the promised land.

The Eucharist allows us to participate in the Passover Supper which all Jews have eaten in times past and present. It allows us to share in the Supper of the Lord and in His passing-over on the cross into glory. It calls us to share in our deliverance from slavery as we hope in the coming of the Savior, Jesus Christ, to bring us the fullness of deliverance and life eternal. Saint Ambrose expresses our present involvement in the Pasch when he writes: "Pasch means the *crossing-over*. For it was on this day that the children of Israel crossed over out of Egypt, and the Son of God crossed over from this world to His father. What gain is it to celebrate the Pasch unless you imitate Him whom you worship; that is, unless you cross over from Egypt, from the darkness of evildoing to the light of virtue, from the love of this world to the love of your heavenly home?"[5]

Divine Energies of Love

In the Eucharist we find the most intense concentration of the Trinity's uncreated energies of love. As we partake of the glorified Body of Christ, we touch and are touched by the fullness of the Trinity. In the Incarnation God so loved the world as to give us His only begotten Son (Jn 3:16). Out of this mystery of His infinite love flows the Eucharist as the "place" where we, individually as this or that person, can encounter the Trinity in their individual, personal relations as Father, Son, and Holy Spirit.

Who sees the Son sees also the Father (Jn 14:9). Who receives the body and blood of the Son of God receives not only the Son but also the Father in His Spirit of love. Who abides in the Son abides in the Father who comes with the Son and His Spirit to dwell within the recipient of the Eucharist (Jn 14:23). Thus the mystery of the Eucharist brings us into the fullness of God's energizing love for us in the resurrection, the death, and the incarnation that returns us to the source of all reality, the beginning of the very process of God's self-giving to human beings in the Trinity, even before creation.

In our oneness with Jesus Christ in the Eucharist we are brought into the heart of the Trinity. Here is the climax of God's eternal plan when He "chose us in Christ, to be holy and spotless, and to live through love in his presence (Eph 1:4). Sin destroys that image and likeness to Jesus Christ within us. Our own sinfulness, added to the effects of original sin, hinders the Holy Spirit from raising us to an awareness in grace that Jesus truly lives in us and we in Him.

But the Eucharist (here we see the need of preparation to receive worthily this sacrament by repentance and an authentic *metanoia* or conversion) restores and powerfully builds up this oneness with Christ.

Incorporated into Christ

Saint Paul especially emphasized in his writings our *incorporation* into Christ. And the Greek Fathers understood that Saint Paul meant this to be a literal union, a true incorporation into Christ's very own substance. By the cross Christ destroyed eschatological death and sin. By His own resurrectional life He brought to us this "new life," effecting a new oneness with Him through His Holy Spirit.

> When he died, he died, once for all, to sin, so his life now is life with
> God; and in that way, you too must consider yourselves to be dead
> to sin but alive for God in Christ Jesus. (Rom 6:10–11)

Baptism, according to Saint Paul, puts us into contact directly with the
risen, glorified Christ who now through His spiritualized Body-Person
can come and truly dwell within us, especially through the Eucharist.
We form with Christ one Body.

> The blessing-cup that we bless is a communion with the blood of
> Christ and the bread that we break is a communion with the body of
> Christ. The fact that there is only one loaf means that, though there
> are many of us, we form a single body because we all have a share in
> this one loaf. (1 Cor 10:16–17)

In the Eucharist we share in Christ's own life, that life of the historical
person Jesus Christ, now gloriously resurrected. Without losing our own
identity we are personally incorporated into Christ. He lives in us, but
we must always be further formed in Him (Gal 4:19). By yielding to the
life-giving influence of Christ, we Christians are gradually transformed
into His image and likeness (Rom 8:29–30).

United with the Father and Spirit

Through the intensification of our union with the risen Jesus, the Holy
Spirit, as the fruit of the Eucharist, brings us into a new awareness of our
being also one with the Father and the Holy Spirit. This is the essence of
the Last Supper Discourse of Jesus as recorded in Saint John's Gospel (Jn
17:20–23). The glory that the Father gave to Jesus through His death-
resurrection is to raise His humanity into a oneness with His "natural"
state of being the only begotten Son of the Father from all eternity.

In the Eucharist Jesus shares this glory with us so that, through the
power of the Holy Spirit, we are able to experience not only our oneness
with Jesus but our oneness as sharers in His Sonship. Saint Cyril of Alexandria summarizes the common teaching of the early Fathers, showing
that our divinization in the Eucharist brings about a union with the
Trinity:

> Accordingly we are all one in the Father and in the Son and in the
> Holy Spirit; one I say, in unity of relationship of love and concord

with God and one another . . . one by conformity in godliness, by communion in the sacred body of Christ, and by fellowship in the one and Holy Spirit and this is a real, physical union.[6]

If Jesus and the Father abide in each other and have come to abide within us in the Eucharist (Jn 14:23), the Holy Spirit, as the bond of unity that brings them together and who proceeds from their abiding union as love, also comes and dwells in us. Saint Paul refers to this reality when he writes: "Your body, you know, is the temple of the Holy Spirit, who is in you since you received him from God" (1 Cor 6:19).

One Body

Not only does the Eucharist bring us into a realized oneness with the Father, Son, and Holy Spirit, but this oneness in many effects a powerful, new experience of our oneness with other human beings. To understand this we must see how Saint Paul uses this term *body*. He usually uses the Greek word for body, *soma*, to refer to the historical body of Jesus which the Apostles saw and touched. That body rose from the dead, the whole Body-Person, Jesus Christ living in His new resurrectional life.

His body is also given as food in the Eucharist. This is a different modality of existence but it flows out from and contains the resurrectional body person, Jesus Christ. Jesus' Body in Saint Paul's writings also refers to His Church, of which He is the Head and His Christian members, who live in His divine life through the Spirit, are true parts of this Body.

We can say that there is absolute identity between the historical and the risen Jesus Christ. The Body of Christ referring to the total Church with Christ as the Head cannot be ontologically identical with the historical or the risen Jesus. There is, however, a partial identity since the very life infusing the members, making them living parts of Christ's Body, is identical with the divine life of the physical Christ. Even though we Christians, in Baptism and the Eucharist and through other means of receiving grace, partake of the same divine life, we still remain ourselves with our own personalities and life.

The Church that reaches the peak of its *oneness* with the glorified Christ in the Eucharist is one in the union between Christ the Head and the individual members. Christ's bodily, risen, human nature is the point of contact between Christ and the Church members. Christ is the Head of the Body-Church, not only by His authority that He imparts to His Church teachers and pastors, but by being the principle of life, the one who gives nourishment and sustenance so that the members can live *in* Him. "... Christ who is the head by whom the whole body is fitted and joined together, every joint adding its own strength" (Eph 4:16).

In strong language Saint Augustine has captured this oneness with Christ to indicate that this union between Christ and His members is more than merely a moral union.

> Let us rejoice and give thanks that we have become not only Christians but Christ. My brothers, do you understand the grace of God our Head? Stand in admiration, rejoice; we have become Christ.[7]

The Eucharist most perfectly expresses the union between Christ and us members in the one Mystical Body. And it is principally in this sacrament that this union is effected. In the Eucharist Jesus Christ comes to us with the fullness of His divine and human natures. He opens to us "the unsearchable riches of Christ" (Eph 3:8). He loves us in the oneness of the infinite, uncreated energies of love of the Trinity. We join our hearts to that of the God-Man and praise and worship the Heavenly Father with a perfect love and complete self-surrender. At no time in the Christian's life is he or she united more powerfully with the power and the glory of Christ risen to receive a oneness to be one Body in one Spirit of love in Christ.

Oneness with Each Other

In the Eucharist we are not only united with the Trinity but we attain a new oneness with the others in whom the same trinitarian life lives, especially within the context of the eucharistic celebration. It is here that the Church, the Body of Christ, comes together in loving union with its Head, Jesus Christ. The Liturgy, or the "work" of the People of God, must always be the context (except in emergencies such as Communion given to the sick) in which the Eucharist is received. The Liturgy is the sacred place and time when the Church is most impregnated by the power of the Holy Spirit. It is the realization of the life of the Church for which it exists: to praise and glorify God for the gifts of life and salvation which we have received.

It is especially in the reception of the Eucharist that all members of Christ's Body are most powerfully united in a new sense of oneness with one another. They symbolically enter into the depths of the richness of God's self-sacrificing love. The Eucharist is not only a sacrament; it is also the ever-now sacrifice of Christ for us to the Father unto our healing and redemption. It is the culmination of all the sacraments as encounters with Christ in His self-giving to us, for in the Eucharist Jesus Christ gives Himself as He did in the first eucharistic celebration of the Last Supper before His death and as He did on the cross.

All of Christ's other powerful miracles and healings have meaning in the light of this greatest power of communication whereby He gives Himself to us in the complete gift. He not merely expresses His desire to die for us individually and communally for the whole of mankind, but He gives us His body as food and His blood as drink. He finds a way to remain among us, imaging always the sacrificing love of the Father unto the last drop of water and blood for us.

The Eucharist is the banquet; Jesus is the Bridegroom. The Church, made up of the community of individual believers in Him, is the Bride. Lives are to be changed. Abiding in the eucharistic union with the Father and the Son, we are to bring forth fruit in abundance.

> It is to the glory of my Father that you should bear much fruit, and then you will be my disciples. . . . Remain in my love. If you keep my commandments, you will remain in my love. This is my commandment: love one another as I have loved you. (Jn 15:8–12)

To Be Eucharist

The divinizing power of the Trinity experienced in the Eucharist is to be the power that drives us outward toward other communities to be Eucharist, bread broken, to give ourselves not only as Jesus did in our behalf, but with Jesus and the Father abiding within us with their Spirit of love and empowering us to do what would be impossible for us to do consistently alone.

The Eucharist is the Bread of Life to be shared with others. Have we really lifted our hearts to God if we have not offered Him our whole being, with our whole set of relationships to other people who touch us and whom we touch in daily life? Of what avail is our suffering in the community's liturgy if it is not completed in the offering of our daily living?

Our participation and sharing in the Body of Christ in the Eucharist are measured by the degree of sharing ourselves with one another before the Father of us all. Saint Paul's vision of the Body of Christ, manifest especially through the Eucharist, shows us to be many members with Christ as our Head. We all have received a variety of gifts but always the same Holy Spirit who builds us all in the gift of love into the same, one Body of Christ, the Church (1 Cor 12:4). Such gifts are to be exercised in love through self-giving. This means that, as Christ went out to minister in love to the needs, bodily, psychical, and spiritual, of those whom He met, so we are to go forth from the Eucharist with the power of the risen Jesus within us to minister likewise with Him to the needs of all whom we meet.

The early Christians call us back to a basic Christian view that can be accepted and understood by persons who extend the Eucharist out into the broken world of which they are a vital part. The deep eucharistic oneness with Christ made them realize the *koinōnia*, the community of all mankind under one loving Heavenly Father. Whatever God had given them they shared with others more needy than themselves. In experiencing the oneness with the whole world, effected by the presence of the risen Lord and the Spirit in the Eucharist, we too can learn to share, as the early Christians did, whatever we are fortunate to have and give to others. Max Delespesse writes:

> The sharing of what they have is possible because they share what they are. . . . Let us recall now only that a sharing on the level of persons precedes a sharing of things and this can come about only because things are extensions of people. It was because the first Christians were of one heart and soul that they pooled their material goods for the benefit of all.[8]

A Cosmic Eucharist

Jesus, the risen Lord of all the universe, the *Pantocrator*, by His resurrection is inserted as a leaven inside the entire, material cosmos. Yet He operates in, He speaks to, He touches, He loves the poor and the destitute. He conquers sin and death empirically only through His living members, through you and me. Those, who have worthily received His body and blood and have received the outpoured Holy Spirit in the Eucharist, are to go out and celebrate the eucharistic liturgy of the High Priest Jesus Christ.

God truly loves the world He created. He looked upon it and saw it to be very good (Gen 1:18). He has created all things, every atom of matter, in and through His Word, Jesus Christ. We are to go forth from the altar of the Lord to witness to the sustaining presence of God's Logos, not only living within us but also sustaining all of creation. Having received the Trinity and having been divinized into their very community of one in unity and many in self-giving relationships, we are to go forth and draw out these energies of the same Trinity that bathe the whole universe and charge it with God's infinite love.

The Body of Christ is being formed through the eucharistic ministry of each human being who acts out of the power of the risen Lord in love. The Body of Christ is being shaped and fashioned by all things material. Our world sees many prophets of doom who point out the chaotic confusion out of which there is "no exit," as Sartre so gloomily declared. Nevertheless, Christians, who receive the Body and Blood of Christ, point to the inner, loving presence of the Cosmic Christ within matter, within this very crazy, careening world. They show that there is a divine purpose, similar to the purpose revealed to them as they reverently receive the glorified humanity of Jesus Christ. The same Holy Spirit, who sweeps them and their fellow communicants into a realized oneness with Jesus Christ and His Father, reveals to them at each step of their daily lives how to effect that same union with the world.

The Spirit reveals the inner presence, now being activated in time and place by the persons in whom Jesus Christ lives, of that same Jesus Christ, as He evolves the universe into His Body. He is moving it toward Omega which He is: "I am the Alpha and the Omega, says the Lord God, who is, who was, and who is to come, the Almighty" (Rev 1:8).

Co-Creators of the World

Such "eucharized" Christians live in the vision of the dynamic love energies of the divine Trinity inside the material world. They seek to serve others humbly in love by calling them to their awesome dignity of cooperating with these uncreated energies of God. Creation of this world is not finished. God did not create the world in the past. He is *now* creating it with the help of human beings. Such Christians in the Eucharist enter into a new creation with Christ risen. The old creation of disharmony and dissension, hatred and self-centeredness is finished for them and now the new age is here as they cooperate in reconciling the entire world to God's original plan of harmony: the Body of Christ, one and many, a unity of all things in the Spirit of God's love with a highlighting at the same time of the uniqueness of each creature, of each material atom.

"It was God who reconciled us to himself through Christ and gave us the work of handing on this reconciliation" (2 Cor 5:18). As in the Eucharist we become more conscious of the trinitarian community and ourselves as a living part of that love-community, we can join the gifts of creativity that God has placed in us to the working power of the triune God, Father, Son, and Holy Spirit.

In humility we will offer ourselves and our talents, whatever they may be, to be used in loving service to build a better world. We will learn to live more and more in the resurrectional hope that is engendered in the social and historical horizontal. Instead of running away from involvement in the activities of this material world, so broken in its "groaning travail," we will learn to move to the "inside" presence of the Trinity working in love at the heart of matter. What we will add to make this world a better world in Christ Jesus will have an eternal effect on the whole process of bringing all things into Christ's Body.

When the love experienced in the Eucharist will become the dominant force in our lives, then every thought, word, and deed will be bathed in the light of the indwelling Trinity inside the whole world. This is all possible because we in the Eucharist touch a part of the "power and glory" of the risen Lord Jesus, who has brought into that very Trinity a part of the material world and a part of our humanity that in Him can never more be separated from the inner life of the Trinity.

The beautiful words of Teilhard de Chardin form a fitting conclusion to this chapter dealing with the risen Lord and the Eucharist as they express the cosmic transforming power of the risen Jesus in and through the Eucharist that touches us and empowers us to bring that eucharistic, resurrectional power to the material world:

> Grant, O God, that when I draw near to the altar to communicate, I may henceforth discern the infinite perspectives hidden beneath the smallness and the nearness of the Host in which You are concealed. . . . Give me the strength to rise above the remaining illusions which tend to make me think of Your touch as circumscribed and momentary. I am beginning to understand: under the sacramental Species it is primarily through the 'accidents' of matter that You

touch me, but, as a consequence, it is also through the whole universe in proportion as this ebbs and flows over me under Your primary influence. In a true sense the arms and the heart which You open to me are nothing less than all the united powers of the world which, penetrated and permeated to their depths by Your will, Your tastes and Your temperament, converge upon my being to form it, nourish it and bear it along towards the center of Your fire. In the Host it is my life that You are offering me, O Jesus.[9]

NOTES

1. Saint John Chrysostom, *Homilies on St. John's Gospel*, trans. Sr. Thomas Aquinas Goddin, in *Fathers of the Church*, vol. 33 (New York: Fathers of the Church, Inc., 1957), pp. 468–69.

2. From the Liturgies of Saints Basil and John Chrysostom.

3. On this point, see F.X. Durrwell, *The Resurrection*, 2nd ed., trans. Rosemary Sheed (New York: Sheed and Ward, 1960), p. 145.

4. Ibid.

5. Cited in *Sunday Sermons of the Fathers* (Chicago: Regnery Press, 1958), vol. 3, p. 219.

6. Saint Cyril of Alexandria, *Commentary on St. John's Gospel*; Migne *PG* 74: 553–61.

7. Cited by Pope Paul VI in his encyclical *Ecclesiam Suam* (N.Y.: Paulist Press, 1965), p. 30.

8. Max Delespesse, *Church Community Leaven and Life-Style* (Ottawa, 1969), p. 30.

9. Pierre Teilhard de Chardin, *The Divine Milieu* (N.Y.: Harper & Bros., 1960), pp. 104–5.

Chapter Six

THE SPIRIT OF
THE RISEN JESUS

Malcolm Muggeridge, the English writer, recounts an interview he had with a Soviet defector, Anatoli Kusnyetsov, who had learned the essence of Christian love in a country where power and brutal harassment invited only fear and retaliation. As he put it:

> Confronted with absolute power, unrestrained, the only possible response to it is not some alternative power arrangement, more humane, enlightened. The only possible response to absolute power is absolute love which our Lord brought into the world. As between Caesar at this most absolute and God at his most remote, there is only Christ.[1]

This Christ has taken upon Himself our sinful condition as a Suffering Servant. He loved us, suffered and died for us that in His *Passover* we might see the perfect image of our Heavenly Father's infinite love for each of us. On the cross Jesus reached the peak of a God-man's love for us. "He had always loved those who were his in the world, but now he showed how perfect his love was" (Jn 13:1).

But it would be only in His death-resurrection that He could finally pour out the fullness of His Holy Spirit. Saint John the Evangelist notes that Jesus promised to pour out His Spirit as living water flowing out of His very own breast. "He was speaking of the Spirit which those who believed in him were to receive; for there was no Spirit as yet because Jesus had not yet been glorified" (Jn 7:39).

Why could Jesus not give the fullness of the Spirit until He had died?

The answer lies in our realization of what the Spirit effected in the person of Jesus in the great mystery of His Passover. Saint Peter preached in his Pentecost sermon in Jerusalem: "God raised this man Jesus to life, and all of us are witnesses to that. Now raised to the heights by God's right hand, he has received from the Father the Holy Spirit, who was promised, and what you see and hear is the outpouring of that Spirit" (Acts 2:32–33).

Raised by the Spirit

In this text and others in the New Testament it is clearly taught that the Father raised Jesus from the dead: ". . . God the Father who raised Jesus from the dead" (Gal 1:2). Yet it is also clearly taught that it is the Spirit who raised Jesus from the dead. ". . . if the Spirit of him who raised Jesus from the dead is living in you, then he who raised Jesus from the dead will give life to your own mortal bodies through his Spirit living in you" (Rom 8:11).

Theologians have sought to explain the interaction of the Father and the Spirit in effecting the resurrection of Jesus.[2] Such explanations will always remain empty if they lose the scriptural view and the relationship of the trinitarian Persons as they mutually re-act upon the humanity of Jesus.

The work of the Holy Spirit in the human life of Jesus was similar to His role within the Trinity. In the Trinity the role of the Holy Spirit is the loving, unifying bond that unites the Father to the Son and yet brings to each of the two Persons His unique personality. Speaking the Word in eternal silence through His outpouring love that is His Holy Spirit, the Heavenly Father hears His Word come back to Him in a perfect, eternal, "yes" of total, surrendering Love, that is again the Holy Spirit. The Spirit "proceeds" from the union of the two, uniquely different Persons, Father and Son. His being as a Person, the hidden, "kenotic" element within the Trinity, consists in being the act of union and distinction between the Father and Son and in this "action" the Spirit finds His "personality."

In the humanity of Jesus the Father poured His Spirit of love into His being. The baptism of Jesus in the Jordan gives us a model of the progress of Jesus' human development over His whole life, climaxing on the cross and resurrection. Jesus receives a vision as He comes out of the water, seeing the Spirit as a gentle dove and hearing His Father declare from on high: "You are my Son, the Beloved, my favour rests on you" (Mk 1:11). The heavens opened and Jesus is made aware in His human consciousness that He is hearing His heavenly Father and seeing the Holy Spirit come upon Him as the Father's Gift.[3] Deep down the human Jesus is swept up into an ecstatic oneness with the Father. Like the water that falls down over His human body, so the love of the Father for Him as His beloved Son cascades over Him and covers Him with His glory. Heaven and earth had been closed by man's first sin in the Garden. Now God's communicating presence has passed through the barrier of sin, and Jesus, God's holiness, stands within the human family.

The Spirit brings Jesus, not in this one moment of His baptism, but in every moment of His conscious, human existence to a greater joyful and peaceful assurance that the Father loves Him. The Spirit gives to the human Jesus the determination to be perfect as the Heavenly Father is perfect (Mt 5:48) and He gives Him also the loving power to fulfill in all events that desire.

By the Power of the Spirit

It is especially on the cross that Jesus receives into His humanity the fullness of the Holy Spirit. There He would be totally inundated, baptized by the Spirit's love in His heart toward His Father and toward all human beings for whom He was dying. "I have come to bring fire to the earth and how I wish it were blazing already! There is a baptism I must still receive, and how great is my distress till it is over" (Lk 12:49–50).

Through the Spirit of love Jesus in His humanity passes over from the weakness of His humanity into becoming in His death-resurrection the full, perfect image of the Father. The raising of Christ by the Father means that the Father is well-pleased as He Himself experiences His infinite love for the human-divine Christ and in Him for every human being created by the Father, according to that image now expressed perfectly in the crucified Savior. Jesus had said: "To have seen me is to have seen the Father" (Jn 14:9). The Father's raising of Jesus from the dead is His eternal begetting of the total Jesus, human-divine, as His only begotten Son. The total Jesus is now the Father's perfect image in human form. But this "raising" up of Jesus from the dead, or the Father's begetting of Jesus as the Son of God, allows Jesus now in His humanity to claim the very name of Yahweh in a new oneness of life through the Holy Spirit. "But God raised him high and gave him the name which is above all other names" (Phil 2:9).[4] Jesus, in becoming like us in all things save sin (Heb 4:15), emptied Himself of the shining glory that was His as one with the eternal Father. And the Spirit of the Father's love was poured out in its fullness as Jesus passed over from the finite, corrupt state of being merely human to the state of His humanity being now gloriously divinized.

Gustave Martelet quotes Saint Paul's text from Romans 1:3–4 to prove that the raising up of Jesus by the Father was effected by the Holy Spirit: "It is about Jesus Christ our Lord who, in the order of the spirit, the spirit of holiness that was in him, was proclaimed Son of God in all his power through his resurrection from the dead." The author argues that in death the human spirit is finite. But if Christ is risen from the dead, He can only be raised by the power of an infinite spirit, the Holy Spirit.

> For by his death man proves that his own spirit is finite. Therefore, if Christ was indeed raised from the dead, as the testimony of the apostles obliges us to affirm, he could only have been raised through the power of a non-finite spirit, wholly other than that of man, and of an infinite holy spirit: the very Spirit of God. Hence Christ of the Resurrection, like Christ of the Incarnation whose profound identity he manifests, relies on the power of the Holy Spirit himself.[5]

Wherever the Spirit operates in the Old and New Testaments He operates as the agent or force of God's power. The Spirit is the creative force of God moving toward chaos and darkness and death and drawing the "void" into a sharing of God's being (Gen 1:2). The Spirit is a powerful wind stirring stillness into a dynamic new life. He is the One who gives new hearts (Ezek 36:26), anointing kings, judges, and prophets with wisdom and knowledge. Jesus received the Spirit as a power, enabling Him to preach, teach, heal, and perform miracles.

But in His death-resurrection Jesus is raised up by the Spirit into the fullness of power. Spirit and power, as Jules Lebreton points out, are closely connected in the theology of Saint Paul.[6] When Saint Paul writes that Jesus was raised by the power and glory of God, he means that it is the Holy Spirit who is the power and the glory of God who raised Jesus. "Yes, but he was crucified through weakness, and still he lives now through the power of God" (2 Cor 13:4).

The power is the Spirit but He imparts the fullness of power to the risen Lord who can now give us a share in that power. "All power is given to me.... Going therefore, teach you all nations" (Mt 28:18–19).

The Glory of the Spirit

As power in the Old Testament is associated with the Spirit, so we find that *glory* also is an attribute of God as Spirit. The glory of God was symbolized by the hidden presence of the Spirit in the cloud. Among the Jews it was through that the cloud was the "place" where God dwelt. This is why God's glory is called in Hebrew *Shekinah*, which means the dwelling. This glory hovered over the Ark of the Covenant and the Holy of Holies in the Temple of Jerusalem.

God's glory comes upon Jesus, Moses, and Elijah on Mount Tabor in the transfiguration in a cloud, symbolizing the presence of the Spirit. Where there is the Holy Spirit, there is the glory of God. Saint John, who writes his Gospel from the perspective of seeing Jesus as risen and radiating the glory of God, can describe at one stroke the hidden glory of God's Spirit which was always with Jesus and the glory that gradually became more and more manifest in the human Jesus until in His resurrection He reached the fullness of receiving God's glory. "The Word was made flesh, he lived among us, and we saw his glory, the glory that is his as the only Son of the Father, full of grace and truth" (Jn 1:14).

Because Jesus has the fullness of God's glory, He can send to us the fullness of the Spirit who allows us to grow into greater and greater glory. If we are united to the glorified Jesus Christ, we are to that degree being transformed into an image of His glory through the same Spirit.

> And we, with our unveiled faces reflecting like mirrors the brightness of the Lord, all grow brighter and brighter as we are turned into the image that we reflect; this is the work of the Lord who is Spirit. (2 Cor 3:18)

Effect on Jesus Human

The Spirit raised Jesus, therefore, and shared His power and glory. In a burst of the Father's Spirit of love that flooded the consciousness of Jesus, the Son of Mary surrendered Himself as total gift to the Father. He knew that He knew that He knew. He belonged to the Heavenly Father ever in His humanity, as the Son of God. All limitations of space and time were destroyed as He moved into the fullness of a new state of being, not only toward the Father, but toward Himself and toward each human person that God had created in Him, the Image. His oneness extended in a cosmic unity with every atom of the universe.

He knew during His lifetime that all things came to Him from the Father. Now He experienced the possession of the very power and glory of God in possessing the fullness of the Spirit. He no longer had any weakness of the flesh, but He is "as a power among you" (2 Cor 13:4), as Saint Paul writes.

The *Last Age* has burst upon the world in Jesus' resurrection. Jesus risen is the fullness of all things, "the first born of all creation" (Col 1:15). "He holds all things in unity" (Col 1:17). He makes it possible for all of us, if we live in Him, to share in His life and resurrection (Jn 11:25). He is the prototype of our future inheritance, the first fruits of those who sleep (1 Col 15:20). If we accept Him as the Son of God the Father, the *Kyrios* or Lord of the universe, our eternal High Priest who mightily offers Himself without ceasing to the Father on our behalf and to us as our food and drink, we shall have eternal life and He Himself will raise us up also on the last day (Jn 6:40).

One Resurrection

If the Holy Spirit was the agent through whom the Father raised Jesus to be life-giving to the world, the same Spirit Jesus can pour out in fullness upon us and even now give us a share in His inheritance (Eph 1:14). The Father raises up only His Son Jesus in the single resurrection through the Spirit.

Thus we, even now, are privileged to participate through the same Spirit in the risen life of Christ. F.X. Durrwell well describes our sharing in the one resurrection of Jesus:

> Whoever unites himself to Christ's body is caught up in the action that raises Christ, is invaded by the eternal Spirit of God: he becomes "one spirit with him" at the same time as one body (1 Col 6:17); he enters into the salvation which is in Christ Jesus.[7]

We are redeemed, made justified and are risen as we share in His death-resurrection of total submission in love to the Father.

Christ Sends Us His Spirit

Therefore, to the risen Christ, who is total spirit and one with the Holy Spirit, it has been given to bestow upon us the power and glory of God's Spirit. We share in the Gift of Christ's Spirit in varying degrees; yet Christ pours out the fullness since He Himself has received of that fullness (Col 2:9-10).

That Spirit forms the total Christ. The Head, that is Christ risen, can receive no greater outpouring. He is risen by the complete and perfect outpouring of the Spirit. As we share in that one Spirit eternally poured out to Christ, we can see that we have no resurrection and no Spirit who raises us to a new creation in Christ, unless we, Christ's members, are living consciously in Him.

Jesus risen is able in His Body, the Church, to share with us His full outpouring of the Spirit and thus to share with us even now as we live our lives in Him the one and only resurrection. Christ and we form one Body by the one Spirit of love (Eph 4:4). We and Christ are the recipients of the one vivifying action of the Holy Spirit.

As Jesus in His risen body, in the total human-divine person, has become a spirit (2 Cor 3:17), one with the Spirit of the Father, so we in our humanity are in process of becoming a spirit, one with Christ. We know what can already be ours as we live in Christ risen by His Spirit. And we can foresee what the fullness will be like as we grow more and more into His image (2 Cor 3:18).

Spiritual Beings

Now we, too, can share in the properties of God's Spirit as Jesus risen does. Jesus was put to death in the body, but "in the spirit he was raised to life" (1 Pt 3:18). "The Spirit of God has made his home in you" (Rom 8:9). As the body of the risen Jesus is spiritualized by the Spirit, so also, but not in the fullness yet, are our bodies holy and a temple of God in whom resides the Holy Spirit (1 Cor 3:16; 1 Cor 6:19).

Leonard Audet gives us an important insight concerning the resurrected body of Christ and hence our sharing even now in that resurrection in our own bodies. What remains in the resurrected body is not the "materiality" but the total "person," which for him is the ultimate meaning of Saint Paul's word *soma* in 1 Cor 15:44. What remains is

Not the soul or spirit in contrast to the body, but a sort of the glorious future man . . . . Soul (psyche) passes away no less than "flesh" (sarx); person continues, but solely in virtue of the pneuma.[8]

This whole person takes on a new "corporeal" body, for we, as Jesus, will always be made up of body, soul, spirit. This resurrected body of ours is already radiated in our present body. It takes on the similar traits of Christ's resurrected body even now as we are moved interiorly by the indwelling Spirit of Jesus guiding us in a life of love.

It is in and through our bodies that we in this life and in the fullness of the resurrection can come to know and love. Both in this present life and in the resurrected life we become human beings, our true "persons," as we communicate knowledge and love in a bodied-being. By now living in the Spirit of the risen Jesus we can experience the "wholeness" of our being as we seek to express our interiority in bodily symbols. We shall discover that our bodies are not external coverings or wrappings around our "souls." But we shall continually experience that our interiority is made "visible," in the words of Edward Schillebeeckx.[9]

Through the Spirit the body of Christ risen and our bodies, now in the *sarx* condition, but also sharing in some beginning way His resurrection, are the whole person seeking to concretize and give expression to what lies interiorly and cannot come forth in knowledge and love except in and through the whole embodied person.

A Resurrected Body

If the Spirit raised Christ and imparted to Him a new, spiritualized bodied-person and the Spirit will do the same for us in our full sharing in the resurrection of Christ, what kind of a "body" relationship is part of the resurrection?

We believe that Jesus broke through the limitations of our human confinement to attain total enlightenment and perfect, loving presence to the entire universe in His resurrection and exaltation. He allowed His early disciples a glimpse into His resurrectional presence. He came to them through closed doors, came upon some as they were walking. His body assumed different forms so they only gradually recognized Him in the breaking of the bread or through some other manifestation. As He could suddenly appear, so He could suddenly disappear.

Saint Paul, as has been already pointed out, tried to hold on to the process of the *already* and the *not yet* of the resurrection as experienced by us humans. He taught that the whole person in Christ in this life was raised up and given a glorious body. The body, again in his thinking, is not a part, but the whole person, individuated and recognized in his or her unique personality, sharing in some mysterious way that Paul does not think important or even possible to describe. He writes that Jesus will transfigure these poor bodies of our into "copies of his glorious body" (Phil 3:21).

> In the resurrection of the dead,
> the thing that is sown is perishable
> but what is raised is imperishable;
> the thing that is sown is contemptible
> but what is raised is glorious;
> the thing that is sown is weak
> but what is raised is powerful;
> when it is sown, it embodies the soul,
> when it is raised it embodies the spirit.
> 1 Cor 15:42–44

Your glorified being will never more suffer or die. Your risen body will enjoy a brilliance reflecting the spirtual wisdom you reached in faith, hope, and love on earth. The gifts of the Spirit will be reflected in your spiritualized bodies' relationships to other beings. Saint Paul admits that we cannot ponder with our human reasoning what awaits us (1 Cor 2:9). Yet Holy Scripture does give us some analogies. "The Lord God will be shining on them. . . . We shall be like Him because we shall see Him as He really is" (Rev 22:5; 1 Jn 3:2). Daniel describes the future state of those in heaven: "The learned will shine as brightly as the vault of heaven and those who have instructed many in virtue, as bright as stars for all eternity" (Dn 12:3).

The Spirit Brings Us Freedom

Thus the indwelling Spirit catches us up in an on-going process of becoming God's children through His regeneration that allows us to be "born of the Spirit" (Jn 3:6). The light of the Spirit leads us out of all darkness and illusion. We are gradually enlightened by the light of His indwelling presence to know the truth that we are in Christ, even now sharing a part of His risen Body. This same Spirit brings us into a sharing of Christ's resurrection by revealing to us that the same Jesus who died for love of us still loves us with that infinity of love reached on the cross as He passed from death to resurrection. "For me he died," cried Saint Paul in a transforming knowledge given Him by the Spirit that dwelt within him (Gal 2:20).

As we yield to such a dynamic love of the present risen Jesus, who is progressively revealed to us through the Spirit and communicates Himself to us in His intimate self-giving, we experience a new freedom of being children of God, loved so immensely by God Himself. Fears and anxieties are shed as we experience new powers to love, to be "toward" God, ourselves and our neighbors. We experience a sharing in Christ's cosmic oneness with the entire, material universe, that brings about a eucharistic sharing as we touch and mould matter into the Body of the risen Jesus.

Freed from sin by the light of the indwelling Spirit of Jesus risen, we no longer can wish to live in darkness. "No one who has been begotten by God sins; because God's seed remains inside him, he cannot sin when he has been begotten by God" (1 Jn 3:9). As the Spirit constantly reveals to us from within our true identity as the full matured children of God, as children loved infinitely by a perfect Father through Jesus Christ who has died for us, we can live each moment in Him and with Him. We can learn to accept our true identity as full, matured children of God as Jesus was.

But this takes place only in the present *now* that is the only *locus*, the meeting-place of God's eternal *now* of His love for us in Christ Jesus. The Holy Spirit progressively brings about our regeneration as children of God to the degree that we yield to His illuminations and inspiration poured forth from within us. These give us knowledge and the power of love to live according to the revealed knowledge toward which the Spirit impels us at each moment, namely, that we possess an inner dignity as children of God, one with the risen Christ, a part of His very Body.

According to Saint Paul, we are alive by the Spirit, so we must walk always by the Spirit. "If you are guided by the Spirit you will be in no danger of yielding to self-indulgence . . . . the Spirit is totally against such a thing . . . . If you are led by the Spirit, no law can touch you" (Gal 5:16–18).

The Working of the Spirit

The work of the risen Christ is to release the Spirit so that we may share abundantly in His resurrectional life. The presence of the Holy Spirit living within us is not a sweetness or consolation to be enjoyed without reference to daily living and growth into greater life as children of God. The indwelling Spirit prods us to enter into the death-resurrection dialectic that Jesus lived as His humanity marched to His "hour." He stimulates us to greater complexity, to greater pruning and inner discipline, all in order that the risen life of Jesus might be shared by us. With Saint Paul we should easily be convinced of our being caught between two opposing forces operating in our lives at all times: the power of darkness and evil and the power of the Spirit of Jesus. This Spirit creates the new life of Christ within us. He also fosters and brings it to fullness in the proportion that the Spirit becomes normative in guiding the Christian to make choices according to the mind of Christ. Ideally we become free of any extrinsic legalism and are guided by this interior communication which we are receiving constantly as we turn within and listen to the Spirit of Jesus.

Saint Paul guides us in discerning when we are following the guidance of the Spirit of the risen Jesus:

> What the Spirit brings is very different: love, joy, peace, patience, kindness, goodness, trustfulness, gentleness and self-control. There can be no law against these things like that, of course. You cannot belong to Christ Jesus unless you crucify all self-indulgent passions and desires. Since the Spirit is our life, let us be directed by the Spirit. (Gal 5:22–25)

It is through the Spirit that God who is love is able to communicate to us the power to be loving, filled with joy, abounding in patience, and, in general, putting on the mind of Christ in all thoughts, words, and deeds. The outpouring of the Spirit by the risen Jesus is the filling up in our hearts of the love of God (Rom 5:5). We are able to love at each moment with the very love of God abiding within us. "Anyone who lives in love lives in God, and God lives in him" (1 Jn 4:16). This love of God through the Spirit gradually possesses our hearts. It is the same love with which God the Father loves His Son and ourselves in Him as His children. We are to yield to this inner power and live in it in all our human relationships. The Holy Spirit dwelling within us is the love of God abiding in us and empowering us to become loving human beings. It is in the power of the Holy Spirit that we can be loving.

Help in Dying

To attain this union of active love with the risen Jesus Lord, the Spirit of Jesus reveals to us how we are to do always all actions to please God, to lead "a life acceptable to Him in all its aspects" (Col 1:10). But this same Spirit, who revealed to the disciples of Jesus all things they had to know about Him, especially the *why* and the *how* of His death on the cross in relationship to His new, resurrectional life, must reveal to us also that we cannot live this new life in Christ unless putting to death our carnal desires, we put on the mind of the risen Savior. It is this Spirit that helps us to live in the resurrection and the victory of Jesus. "The Spirit too comes to help us in our weakness" (Rom 8:26). The Spirit prays within us by allowing us through deeper faith, hope, and love to be present to the Father's overwhelming love for us in each event. But above all, the Spirit pours this divine love into our hearts. It is by the Spirit's love infused into us that we can have the courage and strength to die to selfishness and live to Christ. Thus in the power of the love of God manifested through the presence of the risen Jesus, always dying for us as an image of the perfect love that the Father has for us, we can always be patient and kind, never jealous or boastful, conceited, rude or selfish. We do not need any more to take offense or be resentful. We shall always be ready to excuse, to trust, to hope, and to endure whatever comes. For love is the greatest gift of God. It is truly the Holy Spirit Himself operating freely within us (1 Cor 13:4–13).

To Build a Community

The work of the Holy Spirit is to reveal to us, not only that we are God's children united to the risen Savior, but also that we must go out and bring the good news of the victory of the risen Lord to all human beings who are also called to share the oneness in the only begotten risen Jesus. Jesus is to extend His anointed work through His Spirit poured out into His members in order to take away sins, liberate all mankind from all division and separation, and bring about a new creation that will be the reconciliation of the entire world to the Father in fulfillment of His eternal plan when He created all things in and through His word.

> It was God who reconciled us to himself through Christ and gave us
> the work of handing on this reconciliation. . . . So we are ambassa-
> dors for Christ; it is as though God were appealing through us, and
> the appeal that we make in Christ's name is: be reconciled to God. (2
> Cor 5:18–20)

The Spirit pours out into us, the members of the risen Body of Christ,
the gifts or charisms that are necessary to build up the total Body in all of
Christ's power and glory (1 Cor 12:4–11). There is a variety of gifts but
always the same Spirit whom the risen Jesus pours out among us so that
we can help in building up the Body of Christ.

The greatest outpouring of the Holy Spirit by the risen Jesus occurs in
the celebration of His resurrection in the Eucharist. Here we experience,
not only the risen Jesus in all of His glorified humanity, but by touching
that humanity we are brought directly into a living union with the Blessed Trinity, Father, Son, and Spirit. Let us turn now to see the relationship of the risen Jesus to the Eucharist and our own sharing through that
sacramental encounter with Him in His resurrection through the Holy
Spirit given to us most perfectly in His sacrament of love.

NOTES

1. Cited by Malcolm Muggeridge, *The End of Christendom* (Grand Rapids:
Wm. B. Eerdmans, 1980), pp. 40–41.

2. Typical of such theologians who seek to explain in scholastic terms the
causality of the Father and the Spirit in raising Jesus from the dead is F.X. Durrwell, *The Resurrection*, pp. 92ff.

3. On the human consciousness, see Jacques Guillet, S.J., *The Consciousness of
Jesus*, trans. Edmond Bonin (N.Y.: Newman Press, 1972).

4. See the footnote for this text in the New Jerusalem Bible: ". . . at a deeper
level, gave him the ineffable and divine name which, through the triumph of the
risen Christ, can now be expressed by the title *Kyrios*, Lord" (p. 371, n. 1).

5. Gustave Martelet, "On a Definition of the Holy Spirit through the
Multiform Generation of Christ," in *Lumen Vitae* 28 (1973): 60–61.

6. J. Lebreton, *Les Origines du dogma de la Trinité*, 4th ed. (Paris, 1919), vol. 1,
p. 398.

7. F.X. Durrwell, *In the Redeeming Christ: Toward a Theology of Spirituality*,
trans. by Rosemary Sheed (N.Y.: Sheed and Ward, 1963), p. 256.

8. L. Audet, "Avec quel corps les justes ressuscitent-ils? Analyse de 1 Corin-
thiens 15:44," in *Studies in Religion/Sciences Religieuses* 1 (1971): 176.

9. E. Schillebeeckx, *The Eucharist*, trans. N.D. Smith (N.Y.: Sheed and Ward,
1967), p. 99.

Chapter Seven

RESURRECTION
AND ASCENSION

Symbols are man's signposts that lead him into communication with the Divine. They are meta-rational signs of an interior world that is very real, but whose existence will always remain unknown unless human beings learn the importance of religious symbols.

Carl G. Jung has pointed out that the impoverished West has lost the ability to live with myths and symbols, the archetypal models implanted in man's unconscious whereby he can commune with the invisible world of the Transcendent Absolute. In a dehumanized, rationalistic world, man is rich in techniques, poor in intuitions, in "anima" receptivity to the inner voice that resides in the "temple invisible," to quote Kahlil Gibran. The reaction—to become a person and to continue to grow into greater personalism through inter-mutuality in an I-Thou relationship—has opened to Western man a great interest in body integration, a growing hunger for solitude and silence, as well as an attraction to the practice of Yoga and Zen methods of transcendental meditation.

From Eastern Christianity there is a new-felt influence upon Western Christians through the beautiful Byzantine icons, the Jesus Prayer and the haunting Liturgies so full of hieratic symbols that lead a worshiper into a deep experience of God through vivid sense impressions, not the least of which flow from stirring religious music.

Festal Symbols
One of the unique elements found in Byzantine Christianity is the highly developed religious liturgical feasts that commemorate events or "happenings" recorded in Holy Scripture. The great dogmatic state-

ments that form the basic beliefs of true Christianity, which the West has inherited from the Christian East about the Trinity, Christology and the two natures of Christ, and the role of the Church and Mary in the history of salvation, have evolved from the Christian East. And yet these dogmas were not merely enunciated in the first seven great ecumenical councils of the first eight centuries when bishops, predominantly from the East but also from the West, met to combat the encroachments of heresies within the Christian Church. These great religious truths were also expressed in beautiful, symbolic forms of liturgical worship.

A cluster of major liturgical feasts in the Christian East centers around the fundamental elements of the Christian history of salvation: the death of Jesus Christ, true God and true man, His resurrection from the dead and, intimately connected with this mystery, His exaltation in the ascension, commemorating Jesus going up to Heaven where He now "sits at the right hand of the Father," and the feast of Pentecost or the outpouring of the Holy Spirit of the risen Jesus upon His Church. If we take the feast of the Ascension and link it up, as we find it linked both in the New Testament writings and in the belief of the early Church, kept alive in the intimate relationship in worship of the Byzantine Church with the main feast of the Resurrection, we can understand how to use liturgical symbols to enter into a present experience of a powerful Christian mystery that has tremendous applications for our daily life.

The Meanings to Ascension

When we study the scriptural accounts of the ascension in the New Testament writings and in the liturgical celebration of that feast we discover two essential elements that are not contradictory. First, the biblical texts predominantly refer ascension to the *exaltation* not only of the risen Jesus Christ in all His humanity, but also of the total Christ, the entire human race, into the inner life of the Trinity. This is an "invisible" reality that does not admit of historical verification by eye-witnesses.

The other element found to a lesser degree and of lesser importance, but tied intrinsically to the first, is the description of a visible "ascent" of Jesus, apparently witnessed by His disciples. This is graphically described by Saint Luke in his introduction to the Acts. His intent is clearly to speak in symbolic form of a definitive "leaving" on the part of the risen Savior from this earthly existence, only to highlight a new and more important existence within this material world of ours.

Thus Luke describes the "ascent" of Jesus:

> As he said this he was lifted up while they looked on, and a cloud
> took him from their sight. They were still staring into the sky when
> suddenly two men in white were standing near them and they said,
> 'Why are you men from Galilee standing here looking into the sky?
> Jesus who has been taken up from you into heaven, this same Jesus
> will come back in the same way as you have seen him go there.'
> (Acts 1:9–11)

The important element in the Church's teaching about Christ's ascension is that He has risen from the dead and without any time lapse has
entered into glory. He entered into a new existence, bringing His humanity into the very life of the Trinity. What was hitherto corruptible
matter now shares in incorruptibility. Something of this human existence has been penetrated by God's Spirit of love and so escapes the rav-
ages of sin and death, and now the human existence, the "first to be born
from the dead" (Col 1:18), can share His glory and exaltation with the
human race.

Pierre Benoit well describes this essential teaching of Scripture that
must be retained amid the symbolical language used to describe what historically happened in the history of salvation and is still happening now
in our own personal lives, as we encounter Jesus in His mystery of *now*
resurrection and ascension.

> The essential teaching of Scripture which is to be retained by our
> faith is that Christ through His Resurrection and Ascension departed
> from this present world, corrupted by sin and destined for destruc-
> tion and He entered a new world where God reigns as master and
> here matter is transformed, penetrated and dominated by the Spirit.
> It is a world that is real with a physical reality, like Christ's body
> itself, and which therefore occupies a "place" but a world which ex-
> ists as yet only as a promise or in its embryo, the single risen body of
> Christ, and which will be definitively constituted and revealed only
> at the end of time when a "new heaven" and a new earth are to ap-
> pear.[1]

Invisible Ascension

This fundamental truth that constitutes the essential, revealed truth
about the ascension of Jesus is a "meta-historical" happening. It happened to the historical Jesus as an integral part of what happened to Him

in His resurrection. In the theology of the Johannine literature, the writings of Saint Paul, the Epistle to the Hebrews, and even in the Gospels of Luke, Matthew, and Mark, the ascension and the resurrection of Jesus form a unity. Jesus in this early Christian kerygma, or preaching about the historical Jesus to early converts, is raised from the dead by the Father and at the same time is exalted in full glory and is given full power to release God's Spirit upon His disciples.[2]

The Gospel of Saint John presents the crucifixion of Jesus as already an exaltation to glory: ". . . the Son of Man must be lifted up as Moses lifted up the serpent in the desert, so that everyone who believes may have eternal life in him" (Jn 3:14–15). Knowledge of such an "exaltation" or lifting up of the Son of Man cannot be attained to except through faith. It is a knowing given in faith by God (Jn 8:28). But Saint John also shows the repercussion of the kingly exaltation of Jesus risen at the right hand of the Father in regard to the rest of this world: "And when I am lifted up from the earth, I shall draw all men to myself" (Jn 12:32).

Saint Paul clearly teaches the unity of Christ's resurrection and exaltation. We receive the most primitive account of the bodily resurrection of Jesus in Paul's account of post-resurrectional appearances to the disciples (1 Cor 15:3–8). His point in stressing the witness accounts of Jesus' appearances to His disciples in bodily form is to accentuate the continuity of the historical Jesus with the "new Adam," the risen Lord of the universe. What has happened to Jesus, as a "first cell" of a new world,[3] is in a way already happening to the rest of the cosmos, only to be completed in the *parousia* or the final recapitulation of all things in the power and glory of the risen Jesus.

Yet Paul's teaching is consistent in linking up the risen Jesus and His glorified, new existence with His ability to touch us through His Spirit and allow us to share even now in that same exaltation. Our bodies even now share in the glory of the risen Lord. This he clearly teaches in his Epistle to the Ephesians.

> But God loved us with so much love that he was generous with his mercy: when we were dead through our sins, he brought us to life with Christ—it is through grace that you have been saved—and raised us up with him and gave us a place with him in heaven, in Christ Jesus. (Eph 2:4–6)

Saint Paul presents an early Christian hymn that gives his distinction between the witnessed appearances of Jesus and the belief among His followers that Jesus was "taken up in glory" (1 Tm 3:16). One cannot accept the fact of Jesus' resurrection without faith, built upon the witness of the disciples who saw Him in His bodily form. The same acceptance of Jesus' glorification can be accepted by us only by a concomitant faith in His resurrection. Such a faith allows us to accept Jesus of Nazareth as the "Son of God in all his power through his resurrection from the dead" (Rom 1:4).

The same teaching that links up Jesus' resurrection with His immediate ascension to glory is found in the descriptions of His resurrectional appearances to the disciples. In the Gospel accounts of Matthew, Mark, and even Luke, we find that Jesus is risen and in glory and then in human time and place He condescends to return to appear to His followers in human, bodily form. Resurrection and ascension take place together.

King of Glory

To the author of the Book of Hebrews the exaltation of the risen Lord is presented as the fullness of His kingly ministry. Both the resurrection and ascension of Jesus are taken as His victory over the powers of darkness and evil that have separated this cosmos from God, its Creator. The language used to describe the Son of God entering into His heavenly glory is very much the cultic language of the temple. Jesus ascends to the temple, the presence of God, to perform His priestly service and in doing this, namely, offering Himself as a sealing of the New Covenant with His blood, He is exalted in power and glory. "But now Christ has come, as the high priest of all the blessings which were to come. He has passed through the greater, the more perfect tent, which is better than the one made by men's hands because it is not of this created order and he has entered the sanctuary once and for all . . . with his own blood, having won an eternal redemption for us" (Heb 9:11–12).

This means not only that Jesus is exalted and glorified before the Heavenly Throne but that all of human beings now can share in the same exaltation of humanity entering into the life of God and partaking of the very divine nature. With Jesus who now intercedes for us before the Father, we are gathered up into a oneness in His power and glory. We can be given even now a "possession of an unshakeable kingdom" (Heb 12:28).

This means that the Church is established in history in space and time but already possesses a share in the priestly and kingly power of the risen and ascended Jesus. He stays with us, never leaves us, by now pouring out the fullness of His Spirit upon His followers. He breathes His Spirit upon His Church members, giving them all power. "All authority in heaven and on earth has been given to me. Go, therefore, make disciples of all the nations. . . . And know that I am with you always; yes, to the end of time" (Mt 28:19-20).

All human history is now under the transparent and immanent presence of the gloriously risen and ascending Jesus Christ. And yet this Lord of all space and time (Rev 1:17; Rev 22:12,16) will be seen as He is now in glory: ". . . you will see the Son of Man seated at the right hand of the Power and coming on the clouds of heaven" (Mt 26:64). There will be a final exaltation of Jesus united with the redeemed people and the world they have touched and harmonized into the plan of God through the shared power of the ascended Lord.

Through the ascension Jesus is Lord of the universe and abides among us in His new, resurrectional presence, especially through our encounters with Him in the sacraments. With our cooperation He is effecting a new order, a new creation (2 Cor 5:17-19). And yet the fullness is in the future. His coming through the resurrection and ascension is already accomplished among us. Yet the same manifestation will unfold in greater clarity and availability to the world as the Church struggles to meet the Bridegroom at the end of time.[4]

Mystery and Language

This central mystery of faith in our sharing even now in the glorification of the risen Jesus has to be expressed in terms that can be passed on. We have no other way of teaching such an important mystery except through the limitations of human language. It is Saint Luke, the historian, who presents us with a "witnessed" report of the "ascension" of Jesus to the right hand of the Father (Acts 1:1-11). In preaching of this mystery and in experiencing it in liturgical celebration, the Church has used anthropomorphic images that are tied to an ancient cosmology.

On the one hand, Christians must constantly realize the necessity of using limited human language to express such religious mysteries; on the other hand, they must transcend the limiting elements in such spatial terms by remembering that such images have value only as symbolic carriers of worshipers into the true reality to be experienced in and through those symbols.[5]

We can continue to speak about Jesus' ascension up to a God above us where He sits at the right hand of the Father. Such language is effective insofar as the essential truth of the Ascension mystery is experienced, namely, that Jesus Christ has brought His humanity into a new existence that transcends the limitations of matter. He has entered into the "real" world of God and now has the power to share this with us as we too can "ascend" toward that heavenly realm.

Saint Paul quotes Psalm 68:18 to highlight the true mystery of the Ascension that is, however, expressed in spatial language of a cosmology that was the framework of the Jews and Greeks of his time.

> When he ascended to the height, he captured prisoners, he gave gifts to men. When it says, 'he ascended,' what can it mean if not that he descended right down to the lower regions of the earth? The one who rose higher than all the heavens to fill all things is none other than the one who descended. (Eph 4:8–10)

In Acts Saint Luke presents his account of the ascension in historical terms of an event witnessed by the disciples of Jesus. He does this only to highlight the essential element of the ascension, the invisible glorification of Jesus that can only be accepted by faith through the preaching of the Church. He begins his narrative in Acts where he will describe the spread of the Church after the Lord's departure from this earth. He deemed it fitting, therefore, to describe that last departure of Jesus from His disciples, which would leave the pilgrim Church, not without the ascended Jesus, but with a hope for His final appearance. The departure scene is given to highlight the mystery of why Jesus left this earth, namely, in order to share His glory with us on earth through His Spirit, that in the resurrection-ascension mystery can now be poured out in ever-increasing abundance.

Experiencing the Ascension

By speaking of the mystery of the ascension in the limited terms of human language we must go beyond the mere objectivization of what the disciples of Jesus experienced on Mount Olivet. Just as in the question of the resurrection of Christ's body and our own sharing, even now, in His resurrection, so in the mystery of the ascension we are now in a process that began within the Church at the moment in time when Jesus broke away from the confinements of material space and time and allowed His followers to experience a sharing in His glory. The mystery of the ascension should mean that Christ has been taken into the sphere of the Trinity, Father, and Son, and Holy Spirit. His humanity is forever one within the Trinity. But the Good News preached by the Church in the mystery of the ascension is that we, too, can share in His power and glory.

Jesus is now present to mankind in a new way through His Spirit. The seeds of divinization given to us in our Baptism can unfold into greater glory as we learn to yield to the Spirit of the ascended Jesus. He has ascended, not to leave us, but rather in order to be more closely present to us.

The Father has raised Jesus Christ, His Son, by the Holy Spirit, making the weakness of the flesh (Rom 1:3) now the power of God Himself. And the very weakness of our "fleshly" existence even now holds out to us the meeting place where we can enter into a sharing of eternal life and glory. Because Jesus is totally penetrated by the Holy Spirit, He is the Father's heir, possessing by His new risen state the infinite power of the Father. And by that same Spirit we can share in the mystery of Christ's ascension and experience in our daily lives that we are really children of God (1 Jn 3:1). "And if we are children we are heirs as well: heirs of God and coheirs with Christ, sharing his sufferings so as to share his glory" (Rom 8:17).

Powerful Intercessor

By the Father's gift of "the power of an indestructible life" (Heb 7:16) Jesus fulfills the prophecy of Psalm 110:4: "You are a priest of the order of Melchizedek, and forever" (Heb 7:17). This power to save is utterly certain, since He is living forever to intercede for all to come to God through Him (Heb 7:25). Through this mystery Jesus tells us that He sits at the right of the throne of divine majesty in Heaven (Heb 8:1). His eternal priesthood comes not from an earthly lineage or from any earthly force, but of a heavenly designation that we accept in the mystery of the Ascension. By a free declaration of the Heavenly Father, Jesus as priest is ordained by the ascension to make atonement for our sins, to win "an eternal redemption for us" (Heb 9:12).

As we open up to the mystery presented to us through the ascension, we can by faith received be absolutely certain that Jesus is now with the

Father in His risen, glorified humanity. There He is our mediator, making intercession on our behalf. This eternal sacrifice in the eternal *now* moment is Jesus, who is always offering Himself to the Father on our behalf, as He did on Calvary.

The Eucharist and the Divine Liturgy are possible because of the united realities of the incarnate Word, Jesus Christ, who died for us, but was raised in the resurrection and ascended to Heaven. He has entered through the mystery of the ascension into the Holy of Holies and there He constantly offers Himself for us in the once ever sacrifice that He offered on our behalf on the cross. The Good News is that we now have access to enter also into the sanctuary. We have an infallible approach before the Father. We can now believe the promise of Jesus before He went to His death: "If you remain in me and my words remain in you, you may ask what you will and you shall get it.... And then the Father will give you anything you ask him in my name" (Jn 15:7, 16).

A New Presence

The mystery of the ascension reveals to us the Good News that Jesus Christ is living within us in power and glory through His Spirit in a new and marvelous way, a way in which He could not have been present to those who heard Him preach during His earthly life. Jesus had promised to all who would love Him and keep His word that "my Father will love him, and we shall come to him and make our home with him" (Jn 14:23). The Kingdom of God is really within us. Realizing in prayer that the death, resurrection, and glorification or exaltation of the *Kyrios* or Lord of the universe brought to him the living presence of Jesus Lord, Saint Paul could cry out, "I have been crucified with Christ, and I live now not with my own life but with the life of Christ who lives in me" (Gal 2:20).

Now we can truly follow Saint Paul's injunction to put on Jesus Christ (Gal 3:27; Eph 4:24) and live *in* Christ. Now we have the power to live our Baptism of *death-resurrection* since the truth about the resurrection-ascension can be experienced, as Saint Paul encouraged the Colossians: "... you have died and now the life you have is hidden with Christ in God" (Col 3:3). This is "the mystery of Christ" (Eph 3:4). For this living in Christ we should gladly accept the loss of everything. With Saint Paul we too can consider everything as rubbish as long as we can have Christ (Phil 3:9).

The end for which God created us is guaranteed as attainable *now* through this mystery of the ascension; by the new presence of Christ within us we are a new creation in Him, even now. Now we can live in intimate relationship with Jesus so that His living presence is ever exercising His transforming power in His Spirit of love. If Jesus is so intimately present, He is within us to release the Spirit of love who alone can illumine our minds and ignite our hearts to realize constantly the infinite love of Christ and His Father for us.

Every sacrifice to uproot whatever may pose a threat to this loving union will be made promptly and joyfully. But more importantly, the Christian who grasps the reality of the resurrection-ascension of Jesus will seek to return love for love received. A life of giving of oneself and going outward toward a world community flows from an identity received in the awareness of being nobly loved by God in His Son, Jesus Christ, through His Spirit.

A Cosmic Transformation

As Jesus "ascended" into Heaven—and thus a part of our humanity and our material world has entered into the very family of God—He continually gives us through that union by His oneness with us the strength to live according to His mind. We move away from imperatives and commands to embrace the true freedom of children of God as we strive always to act according to the dignity of children of God. This awareness becomes progressively an infusion into our minds and hearts by the Holy Spirit.

We are *in Christ* as in our true home where we are at ease and live in loving familiarity. At each moment as in loving submission we seek daily to offer every thought, word, and deed for the glory of the Trinity, we enter "into" Christ, to put on His mind in loving submission.

Yet God does not plan that human beings will only be brought into the Trinity. In creating all things in His Word (Jn 1:2) God intends that all matter find a place within the trinitarian community. One of the convictions that flows out of the doctrine of the ascension is that now Jesus Christ is the *Kyrios*, the Lord and Master of the entire universe and that all things belong to Him. "He has put all things under his feet and made him, as the ruler of everything, the head of the Church; which is his body, the fullness of him who fills the whole creation" (Eph 1:22–23).

Through the Spirit of the risen Jesus, we have been baptized into His

Body, the Church, and we are now new creatures. A whole new world, like a leaven, has been inserted into the universe. This new creation is Christ, the Head (Col 1:18). We are members of His Body, the saved humanity, that together must reconcile the entire world and bring it into the fullness according to the eternal plan of the Heavenly Father (2 Cor 5:17–20).

This Body of Christ, the redeemed humanity and the transfigured world brought about by man's cooperation with Jesus Christ, is in process of growing into its fullness. This teaching about the ascension is confirmed by Vatican II's *Constitution on the Church in the Modern World* which assures us:

> The Church, or, in other words, the kingdom of Christ now present
> in mystery, grows visibly through the power of God in the world.[6]

Christ Not Yet Ascended

In a way the teaching of the Church about Christ's ascension into glory can show us also in the doctrine of the Mystical Body of Christ that the mystical Christ has not yet attained to His full growth, and hence to His full glory. He has not yet been raised up by His heavenly Father unto the fullness of His glorification until His members also share in that "con-glorification."

Our human dignity consists in reaching our fulfillment as we work to bring about a world in progress, a world which we thoroughly love along with the love we have for Jesus Christ as we work with Him to bring Him to full stature in His Body, the Church. In the midst of our daily work and as we constantly touch parts of our material world that we have not yet "ascended" to the Father, not yet brought into the Trinity, we can add to the ascension of Christ into greater glory.

The mystery of the ascension and our living in that mystery give to us a penetrating vision that sees more deeply into the material world than appears to our senses. This enables us to go beyond the strict dualism that separates God and the world. If Jesus is ascended into glory and yet is in glory inserted into our very material world, then the world truly becomes a *diaphany*, as Teilhard de Chardin so often describes it, of God's inner, active presence, to form the full, glorified Body of Christ.

The thrilling experience of the mystery of the ascension is that Jesus has promised never to leave us, but to be with us always. Because we believe that Jesus who died really did rise and ascend with his humanity into the very presence of the heavenly Father, we are already in our broken, sinful humanity a part of God's family. The transfiguring power of the triune God, Father, Son, and Holy Spirit, bathe us in their glorifying, "ascending," divinizing energies of love.

Our work and our moments of personal prayer both become "places" of discovering God's loving and active presence as the Father raises us with Christ to a new sharing in His glory. We can now afford to become alive to an exciting world. Indeed, God is not far from any of us, since it is in him that we live, and move, and exist" (Acts 17:28). There is hope for us and our world in that, as Jesus ascended to glory and is one with His Father, so we too even now share in His glory and oneness with His Father. We can believe and work for a world that will be glorified into the Body of Christ.

NOTES

1. Pierre Benoit, O.P., *Jesus and the Gospel*, trans. Benet Weatherhead (N.Y.: Herder and Herder, 1973), vol. 1, pp. 252–53. This chapter on the ascension appeared earlier in French as "L'ascension," in *Revue Biblique* 56 (1949): 161–203.

2. See Joseph Ratzinger, "Ascension of Christ," in *Sacramentum Mundi*, vol. 15, ed. Karl Rahner et al. (N.Y.: Herder and Herder, 1968), p. 109.

3. Benoit, ibid., p. 230–31.

4. See T.F. Torrance, *Space, Time and Resurrection* (Grand Rapids: Wm B. Eerdmans, 1976), pp. 143–54.

5. See Benoit, ibid., 251ff.

6. *De Ecclesia* (Washington, D.C.: N.C.W.C., 1964), p. 3.

Chapter Eight

TODAY IS THE LAST DAY

Christianity is a religion that leads its faithful in a commitment to a person, Jesus Christ. Hinduism and Buddhism teach a way or path to enlightenment. Guatama Buddha is important for Buddhists because of his teachings. For them the historical details of his life are not important. Whether he rose from the dead or not is unimportant. What is important is how to reach his level of enlightenment and so attain the *Buddha* state of everlasting bliss.

To be a Christian is to put one's whole life in faithful and loving obedience to Jesus Christ. He did live as Guatama Buddha. He was enlightened, but He also rose from the dead and now He lives as our Life. Christian faith means that Jesus Christ now lives within us and shares with us through the release of His Holy Spirit His Life everlasting.

It is faith given us as a gift from the Spirit of the risen Christ whereby we *know* in a manner beyond all rational knowledge and wisdom that the historical Jesus of Nazareth is truly the incarnate Word of God, bringing us eternal life.

> Something which has existed since the beginning,
> that we have heard,
> and we have seen with our own eyes;
> that we have watched
> and touched with our hands:
> the Word, who is life—
> this is our subject.
> That life was made visible:
> we saw it and we are giving our testimony,

telling you of the eternal life
which was with the Father and has been made visible to us.
What we have seen and heard
we are telling you
so that you too may be in union with us,
as we are in union
with the Father
and with his Son Jesus Christ.
We are writing this to you to make our own joy complete.

1 Jn 1:1

A Commitment of Love

We accept in faith the faith experience of the first Christian community that continually through the literary genre of the *Gospels* bears witness, not only to the death and resurrection of Jesus Christ, but also to His transforming power upon His followers into a sharing community of people who love one another as He loved them (Jn 15:12).

Such a faith in the risen Lord, who is in the midst of Christians assembled as members of His Body, the Church, is an absurdity according to the "wisdom" of the *world*.

> The hidden wisdom of God which we teach in our mysteries is the wisdom that God predestined to be for our glory before the ages began. It is a wisdom that none of the masters of this age have ever known. . . . We teach that scripture calls: the things that no eye has seen and no ear has heard, things beyond the mind of man, all that God has prepared for those who love him. These are the very things that God has revealed to us through the Spirit, for the Spirit reaches the depths of everything, even the depths of God. (1 Cor 2:7–9)

Belief in Jesus risen cannot be so much a fact that is proved historically. It is belief that calls for a response in love as the Spirit of the risen Lord continually reveals the living Christ within the heart of each believer. Such an ongoing experience in sharing the risen life of Jesus Christ in the context of our everyday life fills us with excitement. We respond with joy and peace as we move continually from life eternal to more life. Death and sin are being destroyed as we experience in the "sacrament of the present moment" the burning love of God almighty, three Persons in a oneness of love for us as individuals and as members of the total Christ.

It is this experienced love of God made manifest to us daily through the Spirit of the risen Jesus that conquers all death-dealing elements in our lives and in our world and leads us into a new oneness with Him. Then in such new life nothing really matters, or rather, everything matters in a new and exciting way. "So there is nothing to boast about in anything human: Paul, Apollos, Cephas, the world, life and death, the present and the future, are all your servants; but you belong to Christ and Christ belongs to God" (1 Cor 3:20–23).

Renewing Power of Love

Christianity calls out a response in love to the ever-present love of God. It is the love of God that is experienced as we die to the distortion of our own reason as the ultimate criterion of true wisdom and open to the wisdom of Christ crucified, risen and exalted in glory.

A symbol of the clash between human reason and the renewing power of God's love is found in Dostoevsky's novel, *Crime and Punishment*. Raskolnikov, a pseudo-superman, plans what he believes is the perfectly conceived murder of an old woman whom he judged not worthy of any further life. In Siberia, as he lives out his sentence for murder, the love of Sonya, a former prostitute, allows him to move beyond his self-centered rationalism, to accept in humble faith her love and then to return it to her and to other convicts. Love had conquered theory.

Opening up to the healing power of the love of another for himself, Raskolnikov confesses that

> he even fancied that all the convicts who had been his enemies looked at him differently; he had even entered into talk with them and they answered him in a friendly way. He remembered that now, and thought it was bound to be so. Wasn't everything now bound to be changed?... He could not think for long together of anything that evening, and he could not have analysed anything consciously; he was simply feeling. Life had stepped into the place of theory and something quite different would work itself out in his mind.[1]

Dostoevsky realistically grasped the mystery of love and suffering, leading to new life as he concluded his novel by commenting on the hero's readiness to serve out the seven years that, in the light of his and Sonya's love, seemed only seven days. "He did not know that the new life would not be given him for nothing, that he would have to pay dear-ly for it, that it would cost him great striving, great suffering. But that is the beginning of a new story." [2]

Love not Unselfishness

C.S. Lewis gives us a keen insight into the essence of Christianity. He suggests that if you were to ask twenty good men today what they thought to be the highest of virtues, nineteen of them would reply, *unselfishness*.

> But if you asked almost any of the great Christians of old, he would have replied, Love. You see what has happened? A negative term has been substituted for a positive, and this is of more than philological importance. The negative ideal of Unselfishness carries with it the suggestion not primarily of securing good things for others, but of going without them ourselves, as if our abstinence and not their happiness was the important point. I do not think this is the Christian virtue of Love. [3]

A sharing in the resurrection of Jesus Christ is more than a negative ideal of never dying as the concept of *immortality* conveys. It is a call to love all whom we meet as we let go of the fears and isolation in the experience of God's infinite love for us. How long it takes us to accept fully the truth that God cares for us infinitely, that Jesus risen lives in us and is constantly loving us with the love of His Father that He imaged once and for all in dying for us on the cross!

We are now in a position to tie up what we have already reflected upon as some of the central elements in the Christian view of Christ's resurrection. Let us in this chapter summarize this teaching by reflecting on two elements that at first seem to be in opposition to each other.

The first is highlighted in the title chosen for this book: the first day of eternity. The vision of the resurrection of Jesus as touching His believers which we find the New Testament writings and the teaching of the early Christian writers and that which we must strive to recapture as we de-objectivize the truth of the resurrection is that *today* is always a becoming of the first day of eternity. Now is the moment of salvation, as Saint Paul taught (2 Cor 6:2) and the only time and place in which we are to encounter the "raising" power of the risen Lord. The end of our pilgrimage and the *going home* is already a state being enjoyed now, but a greater fullness awaits us.

The second area of insight that needs development and forms a most important element in the teaching of the resurrection is that the Church of believers of the risen Savior is a pilgrimage Church that stretches out toward the full coming of the Lord. This full coming of the risen Jesus Christ will embrace not only all of His followers who have lived in His death-resurrection but through them, His *new creation*, He will extend His healing power to all parts of God's created cosmos. In that fullness there will be only the risen Lord, who will embrace all who have lived by His loving Spirit along with a world transformed through their loving and creative powers.

A Now Eternity

Eternity is not what begins when our historical time ceases. It is the everlasting time and life of God that are already the new time in which we Christians now live in Christ. This "new time" of salvation cuts down vertically through our broken, horizontal time that is riddled by what Scripture calls "sin and death." This new time of Christ intersects the old, broken time and becomes a transforming leaven changing historical time into salvific time. This does not mean that the old time is destroyed but rather it is transformed from within the very historicity, including the broken, fragmented moment-by-moment suffering in separation and alienation. It is a gradual consummation of time through the presence of the Risen Lord inserted into the very broken materiality of the universe.

Such a process of the unfolding of God's life, given in embryonic form in our Baptism, is like a seed that already contains the fruit. Still it necessitates a steady growth with each moment's victory a preparation for the next conquest, "from glory to glory." Jesus is already risen, is the shout we raise up, as the early Christians did. He has gone from the world in the sense that now only by faith can He be experienced and "seen." And He will come again in the fullness of glory. But the Good News that gives us courage to live dynamically this present moment with all of its "groaning in travail" is that this risen Jesus is still with us.

He is now releasing His loving Spirit who fills us with love and takes away our fears so that we can enter into the process of becoming living members of the risen body of Christ, the Lord. It is only the Spirit who can reveal to us in any given moment the presence of Christ as risen. This glorified Christ is actually one with us in His power and transforming glory. This Spirit no longer becomes for Christ's followers a mere possession or the Giver of charisms to build up the Body of Christ, His Church. The work of the Spirit is seen in the ground of Christ's resurrection as the Fulfiller of the original purpose of God's creation. The Spirit makes it possible for us Christians to experience the presence and transforming power of the *Kyrios*, the risen Christ to whom all power has been given.

Our Response

Our response to the proclamation of the Good News about the presence of the risen Lord within the context of our daily life but above all to the Proclaimer who is the risen Lord Himself, revealed to us by the Spirit, becomes very important. Our response measures not only the degree of how fully actualized we become as human beings but it participates in the measure of how fully risen the entire Christ will become in the final glorification of "God in all."

The first part of our response to enter into the risen life of Jesus in the *now* moment revolves around a continued *metanoia* or an acceptance of repentance. This is more than merely feeling sorry for any deliberate sinfulness on our part. Those who enter into God's life and live in the Kingdom of God that the risen Jesus is bringing about must continuously turn away from any form of selfishness. As they live in generous love toward all whom they meet and serve, they already participate in the sharing of Christ's victory over death.

During His earthly life Jesus preached the Good News about the inbreaking Kingdom of God. He forgave sins, much to the horror of the religious leaders of His day, as an anticipation of His power as the coming Messiah and Lord of the universe to bring about a new life of God in the hearts of persons who were dead to God's love. The many healings of the sick, maimed, the giving sight to the blind and the restoring of hearing to the deaf, even the raising of the dead to life, were signs of the coming of the Kingdom of God that would come about actually only after Easter. But His believers were living, as we do, in the time of the Lord who has conquered sin and death. The earthly ministry of Jesus was only a partial realization of what is available to us through His continued presence in His Church through His Word and His sacraments, through His loving Spirit when two or three gather in unselfish love.

Repentance should be seen as a movement continually under the Spirit of love of the risen Lord to embrace the *cross* of dying to one's selfish ex-

ploitation of others and to live in loving service to them. It is a movement from darkness into the light of the transforming resurrection of
Christ. This embraces all the elements that the Christian Church has
taught under the rubric of *asceticism*.[4] The end of our Christian life is to
be loving children toward one another since the love of God abounds in
our hearts through the Spirit that the risen Jesus gives to us (Rom 5:5).
This means in the hard concrete details of the *now* moment in which we
encounter the dark areas of our hidden self a "dying" to self as we
uproot the elements in us that hold us back from becoming what we
should be in Christ.

Our lives, also, are to be apostolic in bringing forth fruit of love to
build up a loving community: the Body of Christ, the Church (Jn
15:16). To bear the fruit of love is to remain in Christ. But this means
putting on His mind in each thought. Saint Paul describes the inner
"conversion" from selfishness to Christ-centeredness: "Every thought is
our prisoner, captured to be brought into obedience to Christ. Once you
have given your complete obedience, we are prepared to punish any
disobedience" (2 Cor 10:5). To be united with Jesus risen is the same as
dying to selfishness, but it is positively putting on the new person that
we have become by living in His resurrectional power. "And for anyone
who is in Christ, there is a new creation; the old creation has gone, and
now the new one is here" (2 Cor 5:17).

The grain of wheat must be ground and the grape pressed to make the
flour and the wine which will be transformed into the Body and Blood
of Christ as the fulfillment of His resurrectional life captured in the Eucharist. So we, too, must also die to whatever is false in our being against
our true nature as seen in the image and likeness of Jesus Christ. We
must be pressed by Divine Love until there is nothing of self left so that
we live now no longer as ourselves, but Christ Jesus lives in us (Gal
2:20). It is only through such a death unto new life that Christ will be
able to live within us and we will be able to go forth to bring about that
abundant fruit that Christ has destined to be produced through our humble instrumentality in bringing Him to many others. Through our ordinary work done in love by putting on Christ's mind we can bring the
resurrectional transformation to the materiality of this universe in which
we form a very small but important element.

As we are "converted" by turning our consciousness inwardly to the
indwelling presence of the risen Lord as He released His Spirit of love

within our hearts, it is not only ourselves but the entire cosmos that has been freed from the cosmic, demonic powers that have hitherto ruled human history. As Christ is "the first fruits of all who have fallen asleep" (1 Cor 15:20), so He holds out to us the *promise* of our own resurrection into His one, new life. His is *the* resurrection. There is only His resurrection, the only *one*, and that is His of which we are privileged to share as we not only live in the promise that He holds out to us but as we actualize this promise through our constant state of purifying our hearts so that the heart of Christ can dominate in all of our thoughts, words, and actions.

Our Responsibility

Only we human beings, among all the other creatures on the face of the earth, have been created according to the image and likeness of God (Gen 1:26). Serge Bulgakov, the Russian theologian, ascribes man's uniqueness over all other creatures to his having been made by God to be a self-positing creature.[5] The image of God in us consists ultimately in possessing the spiritual faculties of intellect and will through which we may posit ourselves as an *I*, dependent on the Absolute *Thou* of God. We possess that awesome responsibility of being able to say "yes" to God's humble overture to share His life with us. The resurrection brings that original creation into the full dignity that God shares with us through His Son, who alone can bring us that sharing in the trinitarian life through His resurrectional Spirit.

Martin Heidegger through his teaching of *Dasein* offers us keen insights for a new anthropology that through the resurrection of Jesus can now be realized, away from the static view of the resurrection hitherto embraced by most Christians.[6] Heidegger conceives of us human beings as *Dasein*, a *being-with*. We quest for a *Thou* who can call our true *I-ness* into being. Our full meaningfulness and that of the entire cosmos cannot be found in ourselves or in the world itself but in another. That other one we Christians believe is Christ. We have been created saying a relationship to Him. He is the Cosmic Christ in whom all things, including ourselves, have been created and for whom we must exist if we are to realize our true *I* as we were meant to, in conscious and loving relationship with Jesus Christ risen. The resurrection makes it possible for Christ to be "contemporary" with us at every moment when we wish to surrender to His inner guidance.

With Christ

Jesus' resurrection brings about His Church, His Body extended into the present, broken world, as His followers live with Him and in Him. He is the Head and we are His members (Col 1:18; Rev 1:5). He is the first of many brothers (Rom 8:29). In His resurrection we are already contained, for He is the New Adam who through His life-giving Spirit, imparts to us, His members, a share in His resurrectional reality. The Johannine Gospel identifies Jesus' going to the Father with His death on the cross, His resurrection, ascension, and His coming to the Church from the Father through the outpouring of the Holy Spirit (Jn 14:23, 28; 16:5, 13, 17): ". . . as Christ was raised from the dead by the Father's glory, we too might live a new life" (Rom 6:4).

In His risen existence the full Jesus Christ, God-Man, in fullness of power and glory, can now be in us and we, by His Holy Spirit, can be in Him. Our Christian life becomes no longer a living in pre-Easter time of being guided by the heteronomy of the law, an extrinsic authority, nor by the self-imposed autonomy of our own reason. It is a life in Christ. We are called to live in "the mystery of Christ" (Eph 3:4). This is our prayer that Saint Paul would have us all experience: "All I want is to know Christ and the power of his resurrection and to share his sufferings by reproducing the pattern of his death" (Phil 3:10). We by the resurrection and the Spirit of Jesus are "in Christ" (2 Cor 5:17). This is a shared life whereby Jesus Christ really lives in us as we yield to His Spirit of love.

Discipleship

To be a Christian is to surrender more and more at each moment to the Lordship of Jesus risen. Discipleship is no longer living a static, moralistic life. The ethic of the Christian life is now a living experience of being under the guidance of the Christ-Spirit. It is a stretching out within the context of our daily life to grow into the fullness of Christ. It is to live in Him at every moment as we experience deeply at all times His indwelling presence as an inner light leading us to love over selfishness, light over darkness.

Only as we experience the ever-now of Christ's infinite love, the imaged love of the Father for us, as we experience His dying and rising from the very depths of our "heart" or consciousness, made possible in prayer by the faith, hope, and love given us by the Spirit, can we learn to live in that same resurrection by dying to self and rising to new levels of love toward others.

Discipleship means utter docility to the indwelling Christ so that we surrender to Him the use of our whole being by going outward toward a world community in loving service. Experiencing our oneness with Jesus Christ, we can go out in that union to live according to His mind. We move away from imperatives and commands to embrace the true freedom of children of God who strive always to act according to the true dignity of children of God. This is the *Dasein* or total meaningfulness for which God created us. When we seek to live each moment with such motivation, true freedom results, bringing us deep peace and joy.

Our Christian lives are now a constant inner listening to the will of the Lord to be embraced and fulfilled at each moment in loving submission. Each event brings us into Kierkegaard's "existential decision" of faith, to live according to the mind of Christ risen. Imitation of Christ is not a static moralism but it is a love relationship that is better described as living in the "fellowship of the Holy Spirit" of the risen Lord.

Life in the Risen Christ

Thus by what Teilhard de Chardin calls "the game of the resurrection," Jesus Christ has irrevocably inserted Himself into our material world. He is like a powerful *enzyme*, drawing all of us who freely accept His fermenting love. He stretches out through us, members of His Body, the Church, to touch and raise others into a sharing of the life that we have received through His election.

As we turn within ourselves daily in prayer and purifying reflection that heals us of our selfish love, we find Christ more easily in our material concerns. We yield our talents to His direction. We seek to live according to God's inner harmony found in each event. We become His servants as we lovingly work to serve others. It is possible by God's grace, after much prayer and purification and loving service to others, to live and move and act out of a conscious love for God in the most profane situations. Without detracting from our full concentration on the given tasks at hand, our work can be the environment, a *divine milieu*, in which we adore and serve God who infinitely loves and serves us in Jesus Christ and His Holy Spirit.

We begin to see how the mystery of Christ's resurrection experienced by us in our daily lives and in our work brings us to a sharing in the completion of God's original creation. God is asking us at each moment to work to build the Body of His Son into its fullness. There can be no greater humanizing force in our lives than to work consciously toward this goal. There is where maximum human freedom becomes one with the freeing power of love as we replace ourselves or any other less deity and begin to live in the "new creation" where God is totally loved and served by us.

We are continuously in process, through our daily lives of activities and passivities, joys and sorows, sin and reconciliation, of being "divinized" into God's loving children by becoming one in His only begotten Son. As we know ourselves in the Father's eternal love, we become the extension of His Son's Body, to bring others by our love and God's love in us into that Body.

The Church

God's will from all eternity is "that he would bring everything together under Christ, as head, everything in the heavens and everything on earth" (Eph 1:10). Saint Paul preached that the Church is Christ's Body; He is its Head (Col. 1:18). Christ risen has been given all power and glory by His Heavenly power. This means complete primacy and dominion over the cosmic universe through His death and resurrection. "He has put all things under his feet, and made him, as the ruler of everything, the head of the Church; which is his body, the fullness of him who fills the whole creation" (Eph 1:22–23).

The Church is the resurrected Christ brought into the very materiality of this world, but as life-bearing and glory-raising. It is the Church that is the community of believers who recognize that Jesus is present and is risen to a new, life-giving Spirit. He effects within that community, especially in the Eucharist, a sharing of His own resurrection with His members in whom He lives by means of His Holy Spirit. It is through the presence of the risen Lord as Word preached and sacraments received, above all, as His love uniting all members into one Body, that the risen Jesus touches this world and raises it to a transfigured level of completion.

Ultimately, the risen Jesus will be one with those who make up His Body, the Church. The Church is the result of the resurrection of Jesus, both now and in the *eschaton*, at the end of the ages. As the Church is now and will be, so Jesus is risen but He is also a future promise whereby God will be always present to us in His Word, Jesus Christ, and we will lovingly respond to His presence to release His resurrectional life into a world that is forever becoming more and more the glorious, reflected image of Christ, the Head of the Body.

Eschatology

There has always been in the hearts of us human beings a desire to ponder what the future of our lives and of the entire world will be. Today more than ever, with advanced technology available both creatively and destructively to advance or set back the development of our universe, we moderns are becoming even more concerned about the future. "Futurology" is the science that seeks to understand the future and to provide tools whereby we can obtain greater control over our destiny. The surface of planet Earth is exploding with developing science and technology but there the efforts to harness these skills to develop the earth's resources and to share them with other inhabitants in peace and love have met largely with uncoordinated helter-skelter results.

The difference between sheer science about the future and what the Church has taught in its knowledge about the future of the world is the difference between simple growth toward fruition and the need of something new to enter into the process. Jesus Christ risen is that something new, that life-giving leaven, that has entered into the potentiality of the universe. This is what is called in theology *eschatology*. This is that part of theology that studies from Holy Scripture and the teaching and praying tradition of the Church and raises questions concerning the end of our lives and of the entire world. It is derived from the Greek word *eschaton*, which means the *end* or the last things. It usually concerns such questions as death, judgment, heaven, hell, purgatory, resurrection of the dead, and the *parousia* or the second coming of Christ.

Missionary History

Christ is risen but remains hidden within the Church and the world that is a part of the Church. Yet the Church has always from the original followers' experience of Jesus' first "unveiling" in the appearances recorded in the New Testament longingly looked forward to a full "unveiling." *Parousia* is the Greek word that the Church uses to describe that second coming of Christ in glory at the end of time.[7] There are many scriptural texts that indicate the future coming in fullness of manifested glory of Christ.[8]

But the Church and its members on this earth are caught up in what W. Künneth terms "missionary history."[9] It is not merely a time of waiting expectantly for the fulfillment to come. It is characterized by intense efforts on the part of the members of the Body of Christ to render the hidden presence of the risen Lord more "unveiled" through their loving acts lived in the power of the risen Savior. In these efforts the Easter event is secretly on the move. The consummation is coming about in the sowing, the growth pains, and even to some degree the fruit-bearing of the Spirit of love (Gal 5:22).

But what Christians have always looked forward to as they struggled to bring the risen Lord into His fully manifested glory on this earth was the unveiling of Christ risen from all elements of His hiddenness.

Resurrection of the Body

One of the basic beliefs repeated consistently in the faith symbols not only of the early Church but down through the ages of all Christian Churches is the belief in the resurrection of us human beings from the dead. Faith in our own resurrection is tied inseparably to our faith in Jesus' own resurrection. If He is the New Adam, He rose not for Himself but to share with us, His members, His new life. Saint Paul argues that there is a resurrection from the dead and therefore Christ has been raised.

> Now if Christ is preached as raised from the dead, how can some of you say that there is no resurrection of the dead? But if there is no resurrection of the dead, then Christ has not been raised; if Christ has not been raised, then our preaching is in vain and your faith is in vain. (1 Cor 15:12–14)

But Saint Paul assures his listeners that Christ is really risen and that we too will be raised up with Him. "He who raised the Lord Jesus will raise us also with Jesus and bring us with you into his presence" (2 Cor 4:14).

Furthermore Saint Paul taught that as the Christians learned to live out their Baptism by dying already in this life to themselves, to the *sarx* condition, so they would share in Christ's resurrection.

> We were buried therefore with Him by baptism into death, so that as Christ was raised from the dead by the glory of the Father, we too

might walk in newness of life.... For we know that Christ being raised from the dead will never die again; death no longer has dominion over Him.... So you also must consider yourselves dead to sin and alive to God in Christ Jesus. (Rom 6:4, 9, 11)

The Christian life is already considered as a sharing in the resurrection of Christ. The power of that resurrection or new life should touch all parts of our being: body, soul, and spirit, both in this earthly life and in the life to come. Yet this sharing admits of great growth in this life until it be fulfilled in the "resurrection of the body" on the last day.

Saint Paul, who, more than any other New Testament writer, gave us the teaching about the resurrection of the body, sought to hold on to the process of the *already* and the *not yet* of the resurrection as experienced by us humans. He used the word *body* (*soma*, in Greek) to refer to something that we must always keep in mind when we read his words about the risen human body. He taught that the whole person in Christ in this life would be raised up and be given a glorious body. The body, as we have already pointed out in previous chapters, for Saint Paul and his Jewish contemporaries is not a part, as Plato had taught and so many modern Christians still hold, but rather it refers to the whole person, individuated and recognized in his or her unique personality, sharing in some mysterious way the resurrection of Christ that Saint Paul did not think important or even possible to describe. At most he could write that Jesus will transfigure these poor bodies of ours into "copies of his glorious body" (Phil 3:21).

Neville Clark teaches accurately when he describes the difference in Saint Paul's thinking between "flesh" (*sarx*) and "body" (*soma*).[10] *Sarx* is a description of man in his unity and totality viewed from the particular perspective of his distance from God. It is the creature man as set over against his Creator. It views man in his weakness and frailty. This is his "mortality" (2 Cor 4:11; 10:2; Eph 6:11). *Soma* or "body" describes man also in his unity and totality which no longer emphasizes his frailty, mortality, and distance from God, but as the entire "self" which may be for God or against God.

Thus *soma* may be against God in so far as man's existence in his inalienable corporateness of human life exists in a world captive to sin and death. This is the "body" that is dead because of sin (Rom 8:10). Yet Saint Paul's keen insight is shown as he relates "body" to the Spirit. *Sarx* must die, but man as a total person, an "embodied being" in his *soma*, can receive a share in the Spirit of the risen Jesus and be raised to immortality or a share in divine life. This can be seen in his teaching in his Epistle to the Romans:

> Though your body may be dead it is because of sin, but if Christ is in you then your spirit is life itself because you have been justified; and if the Spirit of him who raised Jesus from the dead is living in you, then he who raised Jesus from the dead will give life to your own mortal bodies through his Spirit living in you. (Rom 8:10–11)

To discuss further what kind of a body we will possess in the raising up of our bodies is for Saint Paul useless. "These are stupid questions," he answers (1 Cor 15:36). He refers the Christians to his basic principle that has been continually highlighted in this present book. Jesus Christ has given us the victory already and our mortal natures have put on immortality or the life of God. As we live in His Spirit, we already possess a personality that is *spirit*. As we live in Christ who is risen, so our "bodies," already as entire persons, even now share in His resurrection and death is swallowed up in victory and no longer has a sting (1 Cor 15:55–56).

The farthest that Saint Paul will go in describing our risen bodies is to maintain:

> . . . the thing that is sown is perishable but what is raised is imperishable; the thing that is sown is contemptible but what is raised is glorious; the thing that is sown is weak but what is raised is powerful; when it is sown, it embodies the soul, when it is raised it embodies the spirit (1 Cor 15:42–44)

We cannot, according to Saint Paul's teaching, even ponder with our human reasoning what awaits us (1 Cor 2:9). Yet Holy Scripture gives us some analogies. Our glorified bodies will never again suffer or die. They will enjoy a brilliance reflecting the spirit of wisdom that we reached in faith, hope, and love on earth. "The Lord God will be shining on them. . . . We shall be like him because we shall see him as he really is" (Rev 22:5; 1 Jn 3:2).

A Corporate Resurrection

What is lacking in Saint Paul's teaching about the resurrection of the body is our usual understanding that is very much rooted in a false dichotomy between our physical bodies and our souls. Resurrection in the fullness on the "last day" in the Pauline sense never refers to the reunion of our souls and our physical bodies. That, as we pointed out earlier, is not resurrection but a resuscitation or reanimation. Resurrection of the body is not a final gathering of raised individuals with "spiritual bodies" but rather it is the salvation of the individual as he or she comes into the salvation of the Body of Christ, the Church. There can be no true development of our unique identity outside of being raised together with all the members into the fullness of Christ (Eph 4:13). This is the Body, the "perfect Man, fully mature with the fullness of Christ himself" (Eph 4:13).

But this corporate "embodiment" into Christ does not imply that we will be less individuals. On the contrary, now we can see how the resurrection completes the original purpose of creation when God wished to make us "according to the image and likeness" of His Son (Gen 1:26). No individual can truly be what God intended him or her to be in Christ without having passed from the *sarx* condition of selfish alienation both from God and from fellow man into the spiritualized *soma* or new bodied being into the risen "body" of Christ.

Christ's resurrection from the dead is the pattern for what we will be like in our sharing in the fullness of His resurrection. From the Gospel narratives we see that the risen Lord is identically the same as the historical Jesus of Nazareth. The appearance accounts of the risen Lord to His disciples are important as the witness of the early Church to the identity of Jesus Christ. It is this man, Jesus, who was put to death, but now God has intervened and raised Him to a oneness in glory with Him, giving Him the title of Kyrios or Lord[11] (Acts 2:32, 36; 5:30–32). The principle of identity that the risen Lord, the Messiah, is truly the same person as the historical person of Jesus of Nazareth is at the center not only of our Christian Christology but at the center of the authority of Jesus on the pages of Scripture and at the center of our own belief in the identity of ourselves in our sharing fully in the resurrection. In the resurrection of Christ God provides the decisive confirmation of the genuineness of the claim of Jesus.

As we believe in His claim to be the Son of God, one with the Father, who gave His life to prove God's love for us, we too can believe that our identity as a person can be transformed by Jesus' Spirit into one who takes his or her full identity in the corporate risen Body of the total Christ.

Cosmic Redemption

As we change our concept of ourselves from individuals who look forward to our individualistic, bodily resurrection and come to see ourselves as already risen in Christ, as we live in loving service to the whole Body of Christ, so we will change our concept of the world around us. No longer do we see it as in the light of the *fall* and of utter corruption but in the light of Christ risen. The resurrection is now seen as the fulfillment of God's total creation. This world does not belong to Satan even though it exists under the *sarx* condemnation and is groaning in travail, as it "retains the hope of being freed, like us, from its slavery to decadence" (Rom 8:21).

Now we can see the cosmos and all material creation as existing not in itself but in Christ by whom and for whom all things have been created (Col 1:15ff.; Jn 1:2–3). If Jesus Christ, the risen Lord, is the first fruits, then what happened to Him in His resurrection also will be shared with His created order. The resurrection of Jesus becomes the inner, dynamic force directing the entire creation to its final completion. He is the *Alpha* and the *Omega*, but He is also at the center of the material world, directing it to its completion and to a sharing in His resurrectional glory.

Jesus Christ risen fills all things (Col 2:19) and is recapitulating the entire cosmos back to the Father: ". . . and all things to be reconciled through him and for him, everything in heaven and everything on earth" (Col 1:20).

It is the Church, like a true leaven, that is inserted into the mass of creation to release the resurrectional power and glory of the Christ by "christifying" all areas of created existence to bring them under the influence of Christ. With man's cooperation the Cosmic Christ is moving this world into a completion. The universe will not be annihilated, but will be transformed into a sharing of the resurrectional life of Christ. "Here we have no lasting city, but we seek the city which is to come" (Heb 13:14).

The *sarx* condition will have to be destroyed. "The elements will dissolve with fire, and the earth and the works which are upon it will be burned up" (2 Pt 3:10). As we must undergo a radical transformation through a death, so the material world must undergo a death or a change to a new and rich renewal. The Christian Church looks hopefully and with patience to a new world that is this world transformed as gold is purified in the crucible of all its dross. "We wait for new heavens and a new earth" (2 Pt 3:13; cf.: Is 65:17; 66:22). Saint Jerome well grasped the identity between the world before Christ and after His transforming, raising power upon it when he wrote: "He [Isaiah in 65:17] did not say that we shall see different heavens and a different earth, but the old and ancient one transformed into something better."[12]

The Second Coming
Our Christian faith has down through history consistently strongly maintained the teaching that Christ will come at the end of time to transform this universe by bringing it to its completion in and through Himself.

> And when everything is subjected to him, then the Son himself will be subject in his turn to the One who subjected all things to him, so that God may be all in all. (1 Cor 15:28)

God brings His creation to a consummation, for He does not create to destroy but to fulfill. A true grasp of the resurrection of Jesus gives us a proper understanding of God's abiding love, not only for us human beings, but for His entire creation. The Christian message is: "Yes, God loved the world so much that he gave his only Son so that everyone who believes in him may not be lost but may have eternal life" (Jn 3:16). It is not a restoration to an original state that existed in the garden of Eden and was lost through sin but it is a bringing to fulfillment of the tremendous potentiality locked in every atom of matter through God's uncreated energies of love in cooperation with the creative, loving actions of human beings to effect the completion of all things in God.

To describe in a word the ultimate end of God's creation, Scripture refers to it as the *parousia*. Jesus is already present in this material universe with His risen glory and power, bringing about the victory over the dark powers of cosmic evil. But in a true sense His victory will be perfect only at the end of time and this is the usual sense in which we use this term. Christ will appear in all of His glory when His Body, the Church, which will be the touching instrument of the material world, will manifest more perfectly than now in this "not yet" condition. This will mean that the Gospel will have been preached and lived throughout the entire universe.

This is a most important teaching that is quite unique to Christianity.

It confesses that we human beings have been meant by God to live in harmony with the entire material world. It professes the belief that God's redeeming love extends not merely to the spiritual side of mankind but also embraces the materiality of the whole cosmos. Man cannot be redeemed unless the world that made him what he is in love-relationships to God's love incarnate in Jesus Christ is also brought into that same redemption. The Good News is that Jesus Christ is already here bringing about the Kingdom of God in our lives and through us bringing it about in the entire world.

We can be sidetracked from the essential elements of this important teaching of the second coming of Christ if we take too literally the scriptural images of life after death as though they will happen exclusively at the end of our human history. To be concerned about how Jesus will look when He comes again to this earth in a cloud of glory to snatch us up with Him to live forever in glory can take us away from the true message of Jesus and His true reality in our present existence. By focusing upon the *parousia* as an eschatological fulfillment that is dependent upon our daily living in the death-resurrection of Jesus Lord, we will be living this doctrine and in the best way we will prepare for His ultimate coming in glory.

Joseph Bonsirven, a noted New Testament scholar, describes this eschatological message of the Gospels:

> The doctrine of the resurrection of the body on the last day is retained, but there is no description of the *Parousia*, or of the signs which will precede the Second Coming. Instead, the emphasis is placed on the element of present fulfillment: eternal life is present possession; the spiritual is already given to us; the Judgment itself is anticipated in the present and so is the *Parousia*.[13]

The End of the World

Questions about the end of the world have always intrigued us. We are curious about what the world in the life to come will look like. We have seen Saint Paul tell us not to speculate idly about what kind of a body we will have in the life to come. The end of the world is not tied to some mathematical equation concerning the heat-death of the world that science can predict to us. It is tied intrinsically to our history as persons who make decisions to live in love or in fear and selfishness. The end of the world is tied not merely to God's ultimate decree but to our human ability to form free decisions as to the direction of this universe. Thus we can never be able to know when the fullness of this world will come and the transformation of this material existence will move the cosmos into a new spiritual existence.

Jesus Christ in the apocalyptic discourses, found in the three synoptic Gospels of Mark, Matthew, and Luke, had much to say about the end of the world. He, or the authors of these Gospels, used the eschatological imagery already found in the prophets Isaiah, Ezekiel, and Daniel, along with the apocryphal writings, such as the Books of Henoch, that were so popular from the second century B.C. through the first century A.D. among the Jews of Palestine. Jesus Himself clearly states: "But as for that day or hour, nobody knows it, neither the angels of heaven, nor the Son; no one but the Father" (Mk 13:32).

The important scriptural message about the end of the world that Jesus leaves with us through the teaching of the Evangelists is that the end of the world is firmly and indissolubly linked to the person of Jesus Christ, who, as the Messiah, the Lord of the universe, will take the Kingdom of God up with Him to share in His power and His glory. He has sovereignty over the entire world and this reign will be manifested at the end of the world so that all nations can see that Jesus Christ is the Lord, the One to whom power and dominion have been given by the Father to unite all things into a loving submission to God (1 Cor 15:28).

The other message about the end of the world, as we have already indicated several times, is the urgency of vigilance in the *now* moment because the Son of God is already coming. He is hidden but already bringing about the glorification of the universe. "Watch, be vigilant" is the message about the end of the world. But it is also a message of joyful hope: *Maranatha!* is the hopeful expectancy that gives us courage in the dark night to await with joy the coming of the dawn of the full light of Christ as Lord. "Come, Lord Jesus" (1 Cor 16:22). With great longing in our hearts we too are to go forth into our world and to unveil the hidden presence of the risen Lord!

Final Judgment

The future final judgment of the world, passed by the Son of God, Jesus Christ, has also been an important belief in the Christian message about the end of the world. Jesus is seen in the eschatological discourse in Matthew's Gospel as gathering the entire world, "all the nations," into a final judgment and a sifting of those who will be "saved" and those who will be condemned.

> When the Son of man comes in his glory ... before him will be gathered all the nations, and he will separate them one from another as a shepherd separates the sheep from the goats.... Then the King will say to those at his right hand, 'Come, O blessed of my Father, inherit the kingdom prepared for you from the foundation of the world.' (Mt 25:31–34)

This is more than a static moment at the end of the world and more than a judgment on the particulars of our good and bad deeds done while on earth. It is in and through this judgment that God will establish the heavenly community, the ultimate state of His Kingdom of Heaven. When God manifests Himself in the fullness of Christ and all things will be seen as sustained in their true being in God's Word made flesh out of love for us, then every one of us will be exposed and seen in the light of Christ. Our identity will be seen in the degree to which we allow the love of Christ's Spirit to create us into our true selves in Him.

The consummation of the world will be a judgment. Those human beings who have lived their Baptism through death to selfishness and living in loving service to others will enter into a life of intimate union with the Trinity and with the entire universe that we could call Heaven. Such will know that that state was theirs while they lived on this earth in love toward others. Others who have encased themselves into self-centered love will be judged to be only that. They will find that their earthly lives prepared them by their free choices to a limited view of reality that excludes God and that is what we could call Hell.[14]

It will be Christ who in a special manner will be manifested as the Universal Judge. "He is the one ordained by God to be judge of the living and the dead" (Acts 10:42). This will be His crowning victory over sin and death. Here in the final judgment do we see the fullness of His Lordship exercised over the entire universe. Here we see the full meaning of His resurrection which is the only resurrection and carries with it a sharing of glory and power to all who have lived while on earth a sharing in His sufferings and death and resurrection to love for others.

> You have been taught that when we were baptized in Christ Jesus we were baptized in his death; in other words, when we were baptized

we went into the tomb with him and joined him in death, so that as Christ was raised from the dead by the Father's glory, we too might live a new life. (Rom 6:1-4)

The teaching about the final judgment is that, as we share in His sufferings through living in love toward others, so we are to share in His glory (Rom 8:17). The details of what it will mean in the final judgment to enter into the fullness of the resurrection of Jesus Christ, to become heirs of God and co-heirs with Christ forever (Rom 8:17) can only remain in the hiddenness of expectant hope: "No eye has seen, nor ear heard, nor the heart of man conceived, what God has prepared for those who love him" (1 Cor 2:9).

Final Glory

If we are guided by the experience of the resurrection of Jesus Christ in our present *now* moment of this earthly existence, we will see that we are already "becoming" a part of the total, glorified Christ. As the resurrection of Jesus describes how divinity and humanity came together in the oneness of His total person, so we can live in the hope that God has created each of us to become a vital part of the one Body of Christ. All creatures, we hope in Christ's Spirit, will share in God's eternal, trinitarian life by being a part of that Body. And that Body will be the source of praise and glory to Him, the source of all life and beauty as we live in the ultimate truth, as Saint Paul expresses it: "There is only Christ: he is everything and he is in everything" (Col 3:11).

But this final glory of the Body of Christ risen is being realized even now as we learn to surrender ourselves in loving service to each other through the Spirit of the risen Lord. The resurrection is a process of the coming into glory of the full Christ. This comes about gradually through the symbol of the cross and death, a symbol of continued purification and conversion away from the dark egoism to embrace and live in the inner light of Jesus risen and living within us. Resurrection is a series of saying "yes" to the dictates of Jesus' Spirit. Thus we become "reconcilers." God gave us the work of handing on this reconciliation (2 Cor 5:18). We have the dignity both in this earthly existence and in the life to come before the fullness of Christ's manifested glory by our service within the Body of Christ to extend the reconciliation by Christ of all things back to the Father.

Jesus Christ is now achieving the victory over cosmic evil through all of His members on earth and those living in Him in eternal life. He is overcoming the forces of death, sin, and chaos and is bringing about a gradual transfiguration of the entire creation of God. But this transfiguration process, since it is energized by God's very own uncreated energies of love living inside His alive members, will stretch forth and yet it will always rest in the freshness of the love acquired and enjoyed in prayerful union with God and with the loving members of the Body of Christ.

The Christian view of our identity in the final glory is not to be the Jewish understanding of a glory that will exist only in the body of human beings left on this earth who will profit from our loving actions while we lived on this earth, as Lloyd Geering so confusedly teaches.[15] The life of glory is both a sharing in the corporate fullness of the Body of Christ and precisely in that fullness finding one's unique, personal fullness as a living member of that Body of Christ that will continually grow from glory to glory.

Love Ever Grows

Saint Paul assures us that in the life to come all other things will pass away except love. "Love does not come to an end" (1 Cor 13:8). Resurrection is always happening even now, as we live in love. Heaven is where God is being recognized by faith as present and as acting in His uncreated love energies as He calls us to respond to His love and to accept a share in the risen Body of Christ.

Moreover Saint Paul assures us that healthy members come in love to aid the injured. Love grows in loving service. Resurrection is love in action. We are sharing in Christ's resurrection as we not only die to selfishness but also as we live for Christ. And this means that we live in loving service to bring the Body of Christ to its full resurrection and glory.

The Kingdom of Heaven is the entrance into the resurrection of Christ through the dynamic interaction of love as we discover God in His unique love for each person whom we encounter. This interaction begins in this earthly existence and continues in the life to come. As we positively allow the power of God in Christ Jesus through His everpresent gift of His Holy Spirit to interact in all of us our power to love increases. We experience the resurrection of the Lord exerting His power of glory upon us. As we grow in love, the resurrectional power of

Jesus becomes more powerful and transforming in our lives. The Body of Christ also grows more full of glory and power.

God is becoming God and Jesus Christ is becoming *the* resurrection as we become living signs of the new creation by the love we allow to shine forth from our lives into the lives of others. We are daily destroying the temple with all its built-in idols as we allow Jesus risen to bring about the fulfillment of His words: "Destory this sanctuary, and in three days I will raise it up" (Jn 2:19).

To let go and live in the mystery of love is to touch the wounds of the risen Lord and know that God is raising His Son to new power and glory. The miracle of the resurrection is happening at every moment of our daily life as we are open to God's Word speaking in His creative act of raising us up to new levels of sharing in His resurrectional, transforming love.

Today is always becoming a new beginning, the first day of eternity, and it is happening as we live death-resurrection in this present, *now* moment. We can interpret the beautiful words, "as long as we love one another God will live in us and his love will be complete in us" (1 Jn 4:12), to mean "as long as we love one another, Christ is more completely being risen in power and glory."

We will stretch out in hope for the fullness of Christ's coming in glory as we open up to the miracle of Christ's living, resurrectional presence in the concrete details of the banality, monotony, brokenness, and seeming meaninglessness to lead us from death to life, from non-reality, to reality, from the darkness of mystery to the light of a new experience in His resurrection.

We already will put to rest the fears of the past and the anxieties of the future as we grapple with faith, hope, and love to discover Jesus risen and raising us to new, transforming love. The new Jerusalem is being fashioned now. And in joy and peace we can say *no* to Babylon and *Yes* to the New Jerusalem, God's new creation. Rooted in the human situation we live in love and seek for that New City that awaits us and yet mysteriously is already here among us.

> You see this city? Here God lives among men. He will make His home among them; they shall be His people, and He will be their God; His name is God-with-them. He will wipe away all tears from their eyes; there will be no more death and no more mourning or sadness. The world of the past has gone.

Then the one sitting on the throne spoke: 'Now I am making the whole of creation new,' He said, 'Write this: that what I am saying is sure and will come true.' And then He said, 'It is already done. I am the Alpha and the Omega, the Beginning and the End. I will give water from the well of life free to anybody who is thirsty; it is the rightful inheritance of the one who proves victorious; and I will be his God and he a son to me. (Rev 21:3-7)

NOTES

1. Fyodor Dostoevsky, *Crime and Punishment*, trans. Constance Garnett (London: Heinemann, 1967), p. 482.

2. Ibid.

3. C.S. Lewis, *The Weight of Glory and Other Addresses* (Grand Rapids: Wm. B. Eerdmans, 1949), p. 11.

4. On the topic of asceticism, see G.A. Maloney, S.J., *Following Jesus in the Real World: Asceticism Today* (Albany, N.Y.: Clarity Publishing, 1979).

5. Serge Bulgakov, "De Verbe Incarné," in *La Sagesse Divine et la Theanthropie* (Paris, 1943), pp. 65-68.

6. I am grateful to Walter Künneth for linking up the thought of Heidegger with the resurrection and for some of the insights here expressed. See Walter Künneth, *The Theology of the Resurrection*, trans. James W. Leitch (St. Louis, Mo.: Concordia Publishing House, 1965).

7. See Neville Clark, *Interpreting the Resurrection* (Philadelphia: Westminster Press, 1967), pp. 63-80.

8. See 1 Cor 15:23; 1 Thes 2:19; 3:13; 4:15; 5:23; 2 Thes 2:1, 8; Jas 5:7 ff.; 2 Pt 3:4; 1 Jn 2:28; 1 Cor 16:17; 2 Cor 10:10.

9. Künneth, op. cit., pp. 252 ff.

10. Neville Clark: op. cit. pp. 67-70.

11. See W. Künneth: op. cit., pp. 111-49 in regard to what the resurrection added to Jesus in receiving the title of *Kyrios* from God.

12. Saint Jerome, *In Isaiam*, 18, 65; Migne *PL* 24:644.

13. Joseph Bonsirven, S.J., *Theology of the New Testament* (Westminster, Md.: Newman Press, 1962), p. 148.

14. See G.A. Maloney, S.J., *The Everlasting Now* (Notre Dame, Ind.: Ave Maria Press, 1980).

15. Lloyd Geering, *Resurrection: A Symbol of Hope* (London: Hodder and Stoughton, 1971), pp. 206 ff.